A Call to Peace

A Call to Peace

52 Meditations
on the Family Pledge of Nonviolence

Jim McGinnis

with Thelma Burgonio-Watson, Gloria Green, Nancy Hastings Sehested,
Ken Lovingood, Don Mosley, and Palmira Perea-Hay

Liguori

ONE LIGUORI DRIVE
LIGUORI MO 63057-9999
314.464.2500

ISBN 0-7648-0215-1
Library of Congress Catalog Card Number: 98-65962

© 1998, The Institute for Peace and Justice
Printed in the United States of America
02 01 00 99 98   5 4 3 2 1

Cover design by Grady Gunter

Contents

Introduction

A *Call to Peace: 52 Meditations on the Family Pledge of Non-violence* is part of our response to the violence that overwhelms so many people and communities. We are part of FAVAN (Families Against Violence Advocacy Network), started in 1996 (see page 118 for a description of FAVAN). As we proclaim in our Manifesto, our deep faith and hope is that we can make a difference through our national and global efforts:

> We join together in this Advocacy Network to express a moral voice, a voice of outrage, that calls all families and our whole culture to reject violence and violent "solutions" to problems. We will break the cycle of violence by creating a circle of families who can be strong and bold because we stand together.

We began with the Family Pledge of Nonviolence as a way of living faithfully in the face of violence twenty-four hours a day, seven days a week. These meditations enrich the Pledge, root it in our religious faith, and give us a way of *being* as well as a way of *acting* in response to the crisis of violence experienced by our families, communities, nations.

This crisis of violence, however, is not debilitating. It is interesting to note that in the Chinese language, the word "crisis" consists of two characters: one means "danger" and the other means "opportunity."

Danger: The tide of violence is sweeping over rural and urban areas, and is threatening the earth itself. The circles of safety, peace, and love surrounding our children have been broken; children are no longer safe. An environment that is supposed to provide safe water, clean air, and healthy food has been plundered and polluted for profit and power. Water is filled with toxic waste; air is filled with pollutants; food is filled with pesticides; land mines scar the landscapes of sixty-four countries around the planet. Children are no longer safe on their way to school, at school, on their way home, where they play—even when they come in from play. They are becoming an endangered species like so many other endangered species on our planet.

Opportunity: But as the danger increases, so do opportunities to confront dangerous patterns and policies. In every era God raises up prophets to point the way, and continues to work through human events to give us signs of hope. God offers everyone of us—individuals, families, faith communities, community organizations, and schools—a chance to participate in the nonviolent transformation of our world.

The examples of nonviolent transformation are heartening. Consider, for example, the growing environmental consciousness that has swept the planet since the first Earth Day was celebrated in 1970. The nuclear arms race finally began to reverse itself as the Berlin Wall, separating the East and the West, came tumbling down in 1989. The forces of racism and separatism were startled by the quick dismantling of apartheid in South Africa as Nelson Mandela was freed from twenty-seven years of imprisonment and offered

South Africans of all backgrounds a way out of the violence that had reigned for decades, centuries actually. People and movements with an inclusive vision struggle with these forces of separatism in the former Yugoslavia, the Middle East, Northern Ireland—in every country and community of the world.

Jim Douglass' book, *The Nonviolent Coming of God* (see page 117), helps us see the significance of our efforts in this broader context. As the tide of violence sweeps across the earth, it is met by a rising tide of nonviolence. In the twentieth century, God gave the world the examples of Mohandas Gandhi, Martin Luther King, Dorothy Day, Cesar Chavez, and countless others who showed us how to participate in nonviolent direct action for social change. Tens of thousands of people joined these campaigns, some of which continue to this day. But now there is the opportunity for millions to join this effort, not just to transform society but also to transform ourselves, our families, faith communities, and other groups to which we belong. This, too, is part of the nonviolent transformation of the world, the "nonviolent coming of God."

In their three-line Native American chant titled "Rainbow People," Mary Jo Oklessen and Susan Stark provide a different way of expressing this opportunity and inspiring us to seize it at this moment of human history:

We are a rainbow people.
We are beams of golden light.
We are the bridge to the dawning of a new day.

As a "rainbow people," each person, ethnic community, and country contributes its own particular beauty and uniqueness to the whole, working side by side to recreate the harmony God shows us in the rainbow. As "beams of golden light," we glow with the goodness of God's golden light. Our acts of love and resistance to violence confirm that the darkness of division will not overcome the light of unity. As bridges to the "dawning of a new day," we link our lives across the chasms of racial, religious, and other differences. We help the next generation move into a multicultural world so different from the largely monocultural world most of us grew up in.

If we consider our moment in history to be like 7:15 a.m. in the dawning process, for example, we can get a glimpse of where we are in the bursting forth of the fullness of God's "new day." Our generation was passed the torch—the vision and the passion—at 7:14 a.m. Now, in this moment of history, we are trying to carry that torch faithfully, at 7:15 a.m., to pass it to the next generation to bring the dawning process to 7:16 a.m. Moment by moment, generation by generation, God is transforming the world. The nonviolent coming of God invites each of us to take that leap of faith, hope, and love and make our lives a part of the nonviolent coming of God at the fullness of God's "new day."

Thus, as you read, reflect, and put into practice the meditations in this book, remember that each prayer you say, each act of love you commit, and each circle of peace you create breaks the cycle of violence and brings God's "new day" one moment closer.

Prayer: *Spirit of God, inspire us to be your instruments in the dawning of your new day. Don't let our lights go out. Turn our flickering flames into beams of golden light. Help us to be your rainbows of hope for the next generation. Don't let us despair that the little bit we can do at 7:15 a.m. doesn't seem like much and certainly won't take us to high noon. High noon is your responsibility. Ours is 7:15 a.m. Keep us faithful in our generational moment, believing that the bridges we help build will be walked on for generations.*

How to Use These Meditations

Organized around the seven components of the Family Pledge of Nonviolence (see page xii), these meditations offer prayerful and practical ways of becoming part of God's nonviolent transformation of the world. They need not be considered as they are ordered in the book, but there is some value in doing so. For example, the first four components of the Pledge focus on interpersonal nonviolence, with "Respect Self and Others" as the foundation of the next three. Keeping these specific components in the given sequence would help you maintain a sense of continuity. It's also a good idea to move through all the meditations for a single component within the same time period, allowing sufficient time to put that component into practice. Unless otherwise indicated, meditations have been written by Jim McGinnis. You will find contributing authors' biographical information on pages 125–126.

The meditations are geared to both individual adults and to families and other intergenerational groups and others living in community, complete with reflection questions and suggestions for action. The meditations draw primarily on the Hebrew and Christian Scriptures but include inspirational passages from other faith traditions. As an aid to prayer and memory, the message of each meditation is reinforced visually. Because there are fifty-two meditations, one meditation could be used for an entire week, filling out the year. The meditation could be part of a weekly family devotional, with the days that follow as a time for putting that meditation into practice.

The songs, videos, and books listed for each meditation might be used during the week as a way to expand understanding of the meditation and its impact on your life. Parents and grandparents of young children will find the children's books (identified as WF—"whole family") and the music for children to be wonderful ways of bringing the Pledge to life for young children. The videos and popular music suggestions are excellent ways to enrich the meditations for older children. The adult books (identified as T/A—for teens and adults, or A—for adults) are a good way to expand adults' understanding of the rich potential offered in each meditation. The hymns listed with the meditations also make the meditations suitable for prayer services.

As such, then, this is not a book to be hurried through or merely read. It is a book to be prayed, lived, and shared. And in that spirit, we ask each reader to pray with and for all those who pray and live this book and link their lives with God's nonviolent transformation of the world.

Note: *Songs from Teaching Peace and Rainbow People are for the entire family, especially families with younger children. The songs from Jubilee primarily are for adults. These three tapes are available from the Institute for Peace and Justice (see Resources, page 120).*

The Family Pledge of Nonviolence

Making peace must start within ourselves and in our families. Each of us, members of the _____ family, commit ourselves as best we can to become nonviolent and peaceable people:

To Respect Self and Others: To respect myself, to affirm others, and to avoid uncaring criticism, hateful words, physical attacks, and self-destructive behavior

To Communicate Better: To share my feelings honestly, to look for safe ways to express my anger, and to work at solving problems peacefully

To Listen: To listen carefully to others, especially those who disagree with me, and to consider others' feelings and needs rather than insist on having my own way

To Forgive: To apologize and make amends when I have hurt another, to forgive others, and to keep from holding grudges

To Respect Nature: To treat the environment and all living things, including our pets, with respect and care

To Play Creatively: To select entertainment and toys that support our family's values and to avoid entertainment that makes violence look exciting, funny, or acceptable

To Be Courageous: To challenge violence in all its forms whenever I encounter it, whether at home, at school, at work, or in the community, and to stand with others who are treated unfairly

This is our pledge. These are our goals. We will check ourselves on what we have pledged once a month on _____ for the next twelve months so we can help each other become more peaceable people.

Pledging family members sign below:

_____

_____

_____

_____

_____

_____

Eliminating violence, one family at a time,
starting with our own.

Part I
Respect Self and Others

To respect myself, to affirm others, and to avoid uncaring criticism, hateful words, physical attacks, and self-destructive behavior

1. Rejoice in Your Goodness; God Does!

For it was you who formed my inward parts.... / I praise you,
for I am fearfully and wonderfully made. (Psalm 139:13-14)

And Mary said, "My soul magnifies the Lord." (Luke 1:47)

Persons who are accepting and loving (nonviolent) can be accepting and loving (nonviolent) of others. Mary sang of her greatness not out of pride but out of deep humility because she realized what God had done for her and was doing through her. She knew the source of her greatness.

The apostle Paul also knew the source of his greatness. He knew he was a sinner, but a sinner touched by God and called to greatness. He understood, too, how God works in us, especially in our times of weakness and through our weakness. "For power is made perfect in weakness" (2 Corinthians 12:9) because it is then that we boldly place ourselves in the hands of God and pray that God will work through us. And then we act and speak out of that confidence. We can rejoice in our goodness, for God surely does! Psalm 139 is such a source of consolation and confidence. Indeed, we are fearfully and wonderfully made!

Prayer: Everything you do, O God, is marvelous, including me. You intended me from the beginning of time. You knew me in my mother's womb where you gave me life. No matter where I go, you are there loving me, calling me by name, inviting me to be an instrument of your love. No matter what I do, I cannot forfeit your love; I cannot drive you away. You will forgive me over and over because you know what I can be. How can I refuse to cooperate with your grace and plans? How can I say "no" because I think I'm not worthy or capable? Your Son Jesus said something I'm only beginning to understand. He said that with your grace we can do even greater things, work greater miracles, than he did. If that's true, it is because you love us and are the force working in us when we yield to your will and do what we can as best we can.

It's hard sometimes, picturing you delighting in us. But we know how much we delight in seeing our children and grandchildren grow. Their tiniest accomplishments stir us; their humblest gifts please us; their courageous or compassionate acts make us proud. Well, how much more must you delight in us, your children!

Living in this love and delight gives me great confidence. I cannot fail even when I fail. You will use my every thought, word, and deed for your own purposes. I am really lovable and capable. And believing this deep down enables me to impart this same truth to others, especially those in the next generation(s). If the canvas of my soul truly magnifies you, my Creator and Parent God, I am not going to throw mud on your work of art. Neither will I throw mud on your other works of art in this world. We are all fearfully, wonderfully made.

Reflection: What do you hear God saying to you in Psalm 139? Put Mary's words into your own mouth and what do you hear and feel? How can you help the members of your family appreciate themselves?

Songs: "To Serve You" (*Jubilee*, see page 120); "You Are Near" (Dan Schutte); "You Are So Beautiful" (Joe Cocker)
Books: *Nathaniel Talking* by Eloise Greenfield (New York: Black Butterfly Children's Books, 1988), WF
Videos: *It's a Wonderful Life* (George is shown how wonderful he is), WF

3

2. You Are God's Work of Art in Progress

Just like the clay in the potter's hand, so are you in my hand.
(Jeremiah 18:6)

When I have fashioned him and breathed into him My Spirit, fall ye down in obeisance to him. (Qur'an 15:29)

We are temples of the Holy Spirit, God's work of art in progress. What an incredible dignity we have! All who see the sculptures of Michelangelo are awed, especially by his Pieta and King David. Yet, God's living works of art—each one of us—are more awesome than a marble David.

What a shame we don't sense our own awesomeness—but we don't. Some of us have low expectations for ourselves. Some of us have high expectations but don't live up to them. Sometimes we engage in self-destructive behaviors that can become addictions—addictions that can lead to depression. We get into a negative spiral and see no way out.

But self-destructive behavior need not take us to the bottom where suicide begins to look like the only way out. First, Psalm 139 reminds us that there is nowhere we can hide from God's love. If we open our sinful, desperate, hurting selves to God's loving presence, God will lead us through. Our "way-maker" God can create a way out of "no way out." In the words of the hymn "Be Not Afraid" (based on Isaiah 43:2-3), "If you pass through raging waters in the sea, you shall not drown. If you walk amidst the burning flames, you shall not be harmed. If you stand before the power of hell and death is at your side, know that I am with you through it all. Be not afraid."

Second, God pursues us in our desperate moments through the loving presence of those who care for us—and through our own efforts to care for others. It's often a difficult call, however. When and how, for example, do we intervene when we see someone we love making big mistakes and engaging in self-destructive behavior? And if we do not intervene, what then?

4

So, how to intervene? We can pray for the person and for the wisdom and courage to intervene compassionately. We can listen nonjudgmentally, repeating what we hear without offering answers. We can acknowledge our own mistakes and sinfulness. We can put concern in our words, our eyes, and our hugs. We must also resist the temptation to rescue addicts from the consequences of their behavior, and not deprive them of the motivation to change. If we are not sure our interventions will be sufficient, we can find someone whose efforts might be more helpful. We can consult with those who have more experience. We can ask for God's guidance.

Prayer: Creator Parent God, you mold me as a potter turns clay into a work of art. What a dignity I have when I realize your Spirit lives inside me. Help me remember this, no matter how bad it gets. And help me convey this reality to others, especially those who are hurting themselves.

Reflection: How might your day be different if you reminded yourself in the morning that you are a divine work of art in progress? What can members of your family do to help one another when poor decisions are causing great pain?

Songs: "The Greatest Love of All" (Whitney Houston); "Be Not Afraid" (Bob Dufford); "Earthen Vessels" (St. Louis Jesuits); "One" (U2); "Everybody Hurts" (REM)

Books: *The Black Snowman* by Phil Mendez (New York: Scholastic Books, 1989), WF; *Winners* by Mary Ellen Lang Collura (New York: Dial Books, 1984), WF

Videos: *Good Will Hunting* (a counselor helps a young man see his worth), T/A; *Mask* (about a youth with a disability), T/A

3. "See Me Beautiful"

Then God said, "Let us make humankind in our image."
(Genesis 1:26)

*In India, when we meet and part we often say "Namaste,"
which means, "I honor the place in you where the entire
universe resides; I honor the place in you of love, of light, of
truth, of peace. I honor the place within you where if you are in
that place in you and I am in that place in me, there is only one
of us… "Namaste." (Grist for the Mill, Ram Dass, quoted in
Peacemaking: Day by Day, Volume 1, page 16)*

Quakers have a phrase to express the divine image in each of us: the "that of God." Ram Dass captured this same truth in his description of the Hindu greeting "Namaste." Thomas Merton wrote that if we could see each other as God sees us, all wars would cease and we would probably fall down and worship one another.

Many teens and adults know this experience of being in love. Our lover often sees the best in us, and we want to be our best for him or her. Grandparents, parents, teachers, coaches, scout leaders, pastors, and others can have a similar effect. Knowing ourselves to be loved frees us to love more than ever before.

It's amazing how feeling loved changes attitudes and behaviors. Accepting and loving others makes it possible for them to be loving and accepting in return. Patient love elicits patient love, and violence decreases. Popular children's singer Red Grammer has a song titled "See Me Beautiful," the lyrics of which capture the essence of feeling loved: "See me beautiful. See the best in me. It's what I really am, all I want to be. It may take some time. It may be hard to find. But see me beautiful."

Such an ability to see the best in others doesn't just happen. It's cultivated day by day in many tiny ways. Visualizing family members being cradled in the arms of a "Grandmother God," for example, can remind us of their divine beauty. Blessing them each evening and saying aloud what a blessing each is to us is a practice that can go on for years. Refusing to think the worst of young people, especially during their toughest years, is important. Making a daily decision to see the best and affirm the best in them is critical. Accentuating the positive keeps us focused on their strengths.

These same dynamics hold true for other relationships, especially those that cause us difficulties at work, in our faith community, in our extended family, or in our neighborhood. Yet, the more we look at the positive traits and contributions of people, the more we are able to work through difficult situations with them. Gandhi developed this ability to a remarkable degree. He convinced his opponents that he truly cared for them even as he fought relentlessly to change their institutional policies and practices.

Prayer: Grandmotherly God, help me see my family members and others in my life as you see them. Help me never to forget how precious they are to you and that you have a mission for them just as you have a mission for me.

Reflection: What steps can you take to see those closest to you as God sees them, especially when they cause you problems? What can you do in your family to see one another as beautiful?

Songs: "See Me Beautiful" (*Teaching Peace*, see page 120); "Ship in the Harbor" (*Rainbow People* lullaby, see page 120); "Beautiful People" (Melonie); "Dwelling Place" (John Foley)

Books: *Designed by God, So I Must Be Special* by Bonnie Sose (Orlando, FL: Character Builders for Kids, 1988), WF

Videos: *Washington Square* (a father's inability to see his daughter as beautiful), T/A; *The Spitfire Grill* (a coming to see another as beautiful), T/A

4. Fan Their Flickering Flames

A bruised reed he will not break, and a flickering flame he will not quench. (Isaiah 42:3, paraphrased)

Breathing in, I calm my body. Breathing out, I smile. Dwelling in the present moment, I know this is a wonderful moment. (Thich Nhat Hanh, *Present Moment, Wonderful Moment*)

"Let the little children come to me." (Luke 18:16)

People with low self-esteem generally find it difficult, if not impossible, to be sensitive to others, to care for others, to take risks for others, or to embrace diversity of any kind. In conflict situations these people usually resort to fight or flight before they attempt nonviolent alternatives. Conversely, people who feel respected and affirmed are better able to do all the above.

Isaiah reminds us that the Messiah will be someone who doesn't break bruised reeds or quench flickering flames. If we think of the young people in our lives as "flickering flames," we are all too well aware of how we can quench their flickering flames. But we also know that we have the power to fan their flickering flames. Like Jesus, we can welcome children and consciously work at building their self-esteem. There are so many ways to do this.

We can give lots of verbal praise to young people, for example, not just for successes but for their fine efforts. Written affirmations are often more effective—whether in the form of notes, letters, or bracelets (necklaces) made of paper chain links on which we write the ways the recipient is a real "jewel." Loving touches, pats on the back, and a wide assortment of hugs are indispensable. Giving others our full attention and listening with both eyes and ears tell young people they are special. Asking for their opinions, giving them responsibilities and choices, and always using their names with respect add further possibilities. Singing to others reinforces their sense of being special, and smiling at others works wonders. In fact, the famous Buddhist peacemaker and spiritual guide Thich Nhat Hanh calls smiling the most basic peace work. Smiling can transform situations as well as individual hearts and attitudes. Our love radiates first through our eyes, which is why Francis of Assisi used to speak of loving people with your eyes. My children once told me I had a face that said "No." I know that face; it intimidates rather than invites. Smiling, on the other hand, says "Yes, you're special." Sending family members off to work and school each day with a smile, a hug, and an affirming word or sign makes a huge difference in how they will relate and perform throughout the day. Receiving one another at home at the end of the day in a similar way has similar results.

Smiles and affirming words can also transform those random encounters we have with people in stores, on the bus, on the street, in the elevator—wherever people cross paths. Fanning flickering flames is always appreciated, effective, and can even be contagious.

Prayer: Jesus, you had kind words for everyone but hypocrites. Help me soften my face, words, and touch. Help me put a smile on my face and a song in my heart. Help me to radiate your love to others. May I never be too busy to welcome a child as you did.

Reflection: How can you fan the flickering flames in your life? How can you make your home a more affirming place?

Songs: "I Think You're Wonderful" (*Teaching Peace*, see page 120); "Part of the Family" (*Jubilee*, see page 120); "When You're Smiling" (traditional); "Like a Child" (Jars of Clay) **Books:** *Mama, Do You Love Me?* by Barbara Joosse (San Francisco: Chronicle Books, 1991), WF **Videos:** *Dead Poets' Society* (the power of teachers and parents to fan and quench flickering flames), T/A; *The Great Santini* (a mother's affirming letter to her son), T/A

9

5. Respect Women

Husbands, love your wives and never treat them harshly.
(Colossians 3:19)

And reverence the wombs that bore you. (Qur'an 4:1)

*"How is it that you, a Jew, ask a drink of me, a woman of
Samaria?"...Just then his disciples came. They were astonished
that he was speaking with a woman.* (John 4:9,27)

What a sad situation the human family faces when such an
obvious dictum—"husbands, never treat your wives
harshly"—is violated so widely. The violence men do in war, on
the streets, to the environment, in corporate board rooms, even in the
sports they play, has invaded the home, supposedly a sacred place of
safety. Not that there has never been domestic violence in human
history, but its level of severity seems greater than ever before. Yet,
Jesus calls us to a much higher standard than merely "don't
abuse her." The love that husbands should have for their wives—
actually, the love all friends should have for one another—is shown
by Jesus' total giving of his life for others. Such respect and love for
another means we would give even our life for the well-being of
others.

Jesus' conversation with the Samaritan woman breaks down a
huge social barrier of his time. It startles his disciples, but also
starts a badly needed change. Men must begin to respect women
as equals—as partners in marriage, in the work place, at worship,
on committees, wherever. No one should expect to be waited on
by others because of their gender; both men and women should
wait on others. Both should be willing to make sacrifices in their
daily routines to care for others. Men should accord the opinions
and insights of women as no less valid than those of men. Men
should not assume that they get to eat first, speak first, or be the
final decision-maker. These are areas of mutuality, partnership.
As a way of making reparation for all their years of domination
and as a way of learning new habits and attitudes, men might
consciously decide to be the last to choose at meal time and the

last to speak in a group. They might defer, whenever possible, to the desires and preferences of others.

Again, Jesus is our model, perhaps most graphically when he gets down on his knees and washes the feet of his disciples. For men who are used to having women do the serving and "dirty work"—changing diapers, cleaning toilets, running errands, cooking—this calls for a dramatic change in attitude and behavior. But there are so many opportunities, every day, to act our way into a new way of thinking.

Prayer: Jesus, your attitudes toward women and service are sorely needed in our own time. Help us men to see the errors and arrogance of our ways. Help us women to find the courage to command the respect we deserve. Help all of us to find the patience to grow together into a new way of being, a way that models your own sacrificial love.

Reflection: What situations offer you opportunities to give or command the respect women deserve? How can you distribute the household and child-rearing tasks more equitably in your family? How can you encourage respect for women in the boys and (other) men in your family?

Songs: "The Woman at the Well" (traditional); "Beginning Today" (Dameans); "Bread and Roses" (traditional)
Books: *The Woman Who Outshone the Sun; La Mujer Que Brillaba Aun Mas Que el Sol* by Alejandro Cruz Martinez (San Francisco: Children's Book Press, 1991), WF
Videos: *Eleni* (a Greek peasant woman tells her own mother she is tired of living in the shadow of men) T/A

6. Respect Parents and Elders
Palmira Perea-Hay

For a [parent's] blessing strengthens / the houses of the children.... / The glory of one's [parents] is one's own glory, / and it is a disgrace for children not to respect their [parents]. (Sirach 3:9,11)

Be kind to parents. Whether one or both of them attain old age in thy life, say not to them a word of contempt, nor repel them; but address them in terms of honor. (Qur'an 17:23)

These passages counsel us to respect our parents in word and in deed so that a great blessing may come from them. But when I was young and heard readings like these from Scripture, I always felt rebellious, especially during my teen years. I felt that if I was mandated to respect my elders, they should be mandated to do likewise toward me!

Now I realize what a blessing my mother and father were for me—then and now. While my mother died when I was only twenty-four years old, I count it as one of God's long-lived blessings that my ninety-two-year-old father is still living. My six brothers and sisters and I are united in providing him with the best care and love we can during these final stages of his life.

In our Hispanic culture, *respeto*, or deep love and respect for our elders, has been well ingrained in our psyche. Having my father with us for all these years has been a blessing I never want to forget. Though my father has full-time caregivers who have been secured through the cooperation of all members of the family, one of my brothers or sisters visits him every day. On weekends, there is a schedule for the preparation and delivery of his noon meal.

We have often talked about the times we got a blessing from our parents each night before retiring. As we were growing up, we had the custom of going to Mother and Father and asking for a blessing (*la bendición*). They would always touch us and make the Sign of the Cross on our forehead. Even if all day we were busy about many things, that one moment of touch and blessing did much to make us feel special.

Deep down, each of us senses our worth and our dignity. It is this same healthy self-love and self-respect that lets us extend ourselves to our fellow human beings who are sharing our earthly journey. The passages above apply not just to one's parents but to all human beings. We are challenged to respect all persons and find a blessing in each of our fellow human beings.

Prayer: I praise you God, my Creator, for I am wonderfully made! I praise you, too, for my wonderful companions in this journey toward you, especially those in my own family. Help me always treat others with the respect which I so much want from them.

Reflection: Who are the elders in your life? How could you show them more respect? Do you have a blessing ritual in your family? Some families have a nightly blessing. Others might have one upon leaving or returning home. If you do not have a family blessing, would now be a good time to start one?

Songs: "The Living Years" (Mike and the Mechanics); "Leader of the Band" (Dan Fogelberg)

Books: *Sachiko Means Happiness* by Kimiko Sakai (San Francisco: Children's Book Press, 1990), WF

Videos: *Avalon* (a portrayal of deep bonds across three generations), T/A

7. The Courage to Expect Respect
Gloria Green

For in the one Spirit we were all baptized into one body—Jews or Greeks, slaves or free—and we were all made to drink of one Spirit. (1 Corinthians 12:13)

I always taught my five children to be responsible and take care of themselves. One Christmas my children saved their money to buy gifts, and I took them shopping. They selected what they wanted and went to stand at the counter to pay for their selections. The sales clerk looked at them and then looked away. When another woman came up to the counter to pay for her selections, the sales clerk walked past my children to wait on her. At that point, I stepped up to the counter and asked the clerk if she had seen the children standing there. She replied, "Oh, I didn't know they wanted to buy something." I informed her that we could report her and added that the next time she sees children at the counter, she should not dismiss them as if they did not exist.

I then turned to the children and told them that there were other stores where they could shop; they didn't have to buy anything at this particular store. The children thought about it briefly and decided to go somewhere else. I was proud of their courage. As children, they could and did make a decision not to allow themselves to be disrespected. Respecting themselves, they were able to assert their dignity to others.

At the next store, the sales clerk allowed the children plenty of time and even let them smell the perfume to be sure it was what they wanted. She talked to them about doing their own shopping and how she thought they were very mature for their ages. The children felt proud about taking responsibility for buying their own gifts and courageous about choosing to shop where they would be respected. On the way home, they discussed how they wanted to give people the same respect the sales clerk in the second store had given them. I explained to them that they should always treat people with respect, but should also have the courage to speak out when they are disrespected.

As an African-American woman, I have had to expect and demand respect many times. I realize that I am not alone in this. Many others face similar challenges—women of any color, many youth, lesbians and gays, homeless people, people whose body shapes or disabilities make them stand out as "different." We are all different. We all have beauty and dignity because we are all equally unique children of God.

Prayer: Lord Jesus, lead me, guide me, along the way. If you lead me, I cannot stray. Let me walk each day with thee. Lead me, O Lord, lead me. Help me tread in the paths of righteousness. Be my aid when sin and others oppress me or those dear to me. I put all my trust in thee. Lead me, O Lord, lead me.

Reflection: In what ways do people disrespect one another? How can members of your family stand up for others who are being disrespected? How can members of your family stand up for themselves when they are being disrespected?

Songs: "Lead Me, Guide Me" (Doris M. Akers); "They'll Know We Are Christians by Our Love" (Peter Scholtes)
Books: *The Friendship* by Mildred Taylor (New York: Dial Books, 1987), WF

Rosa Parks at Peace Abbey

Videos: *Long Walk Home* (a fictional account of the Montgomery bus boycott), T/A; *Amistad* (the historical retelling of slaves revolting, demanding their freedom), T/A; *Philadelphia* (the struggles of a gay person), T/A

Part 11
Communicate Better

To share my feelings honestly, to look for safe ways to express my anger, and to work at solving problems peacefully

1. Nonviolence as Mutuality

Be subject to one another out of reverence for Christ.
(Ephesians 5:21)

"Whoever wishes to become great among you must be your servant." (Mark 10:43)

Then he poured water into a basin and began to wash the disciples' feet....I have set you an example, that you also should do as I have done to you." (John 13:5,15)

W e are created in the image and likeness of a God who is a mutuality of three equal Persons. As such, God is more fully imaged in human structures by mutual relationships, not hierarchical or vertical ones (which often lead to domination by the one or ones on top).

One of the gifts of the twentieth century to human evolution is the awareness of the need—and the intensification of the struggle—to turn dominating, vertical relationships into horizontal, mutual partnerships. This is true at all levels of relationships—interpersonal relationships, family relationships, work place relationships, international relationships, and even our relationship with the earth.

Jesus' understanding of authority as service applies to all realms of living, beginning with the family. But Jesus' example of horizontal living is even more dramatic. He gets down on his knees and washes the feet of his disciples and tells them to follow his example. Then, less than twenty-four hours later, he stretches forth his arms in an act of total love.

Yes, spouses are called to be subject to each other and to lay down their lives for each other, as parents are called to do so for their children. One way to sacrifice ourselves daily is by letting go of control over others and creating more horizontal decision-making processes wherever we are in leadership. At home this means all family members participate in decisions to the extent that they are able. Family meetings, for example, offer opportunities to discuss plans that affect the entire family and to reach mutual resolutions to family conflicts. Family meetings can also address family service (helping others), family fun, and family celebrations. Everyone participates; no one dominates. Participatory relationships, processes, and structures are nonviolent. Dominating ones are violent.

One of the best ways to imagine the strength of mutuality is to envision a circle where no point is first or last; all points are equal. This is true for families; all members are equal, although the roles may be different. "Creating circles of peace to break the cycle of violence" is more than a slogan. Circles of peace truly do break the cycle of violence. Some teachers form sharing circles in their classrooms. Some families form circles for their family meetings and meals. One Native American family uses a "peace rug" for their family meetings; family members sit on it in a circle whenever anyone feels the need to gather the whole family for a discussion or decision.

Prayer: Jesus, help us get off our pedestals of power and privilege and begin serving and relating to others as you did. Help us reflect the Godhead, in whose image we have been created, by striving to transform our relationships into genuine partnerships. Help us daily to promote your beloved community by each act of mutuality we do.

Reflection: What vertical relationships or structures do you find yourself in? What is one thing you can do in one of these situations to make it more horizontal or circular? How can you make your family a "circle" to help break the cycle of violence?

Songs: "With Two Wings" (*Teaching Peace*, see page 120); "What Does the Lord Require?" (*Jubilee*, see page 120); "Where Charity and Love Prevail" (Paul Benoit); "May the Circle Be Unbroken" (Johnny Cash)

Books: *Free To Be You and Me* by Marlo Thomas (New York: McGraw Hill, 1974), WF
Videos: *The Great Santini* (a son's struggle toward mutuality with his tyrannical father), T/A; *Free To Be You and Me* (video version of the book), WF

19

2. Good Communication Begins in Silence

But I have calmed and quieted my soul, / like a weaned child with its mother; / my soul is like the weaned child that is with me. (Psalm 131:2)

Let everyone be quick to listen, slow to speak, slow to anger. (James 1:19)

Block your mouth, shut the doors of eyes and ears, and you will have fullness within. Open your mouth, be always busy, and you're beyond hope! (Lao Tzu, *Tao Te Ching*, quoted in *The Fire of Silence and Stillness: An Anthology of Quotations for the Spiritual Journey*, edited by Paul Harris; London: Darton, Longman, & Todd Ltd., 1995)

So many fights are ignited and/or fueled with thoughtless remarks. How often we react without thinking. And once our words fan the flames of discord, it's too late to take them back.

Listening carefully before speaking is a difficult discipline to learn, but we can learn. My wife, Kathy, is the master of listening in our family. She consistently does three things. First, she says "We'll think about it" rather than offering an immediate "No!" This gives us time to think through our children's request, to pray about it, and to talk with other parents about it if need be. In the end, our response is more thoughtful and generally better received by our children. Second, she bites her tongue and does not comment or pass judgment on what she's being told. Eye contact and an occasional "I see" or "Uh-huh" assures our children that she hears what is being said. Finally, she paraphrases; she feeds back what she hears. She acknowledges feelings and facts with statements like "I sense you're pretty upset because you think your girlfriend isn't at the same place you are."

There are so many times, in our roles as parents and in other situations, when we jump to conclusions before hearing enough and probing enough. I like to remind myself that God gave me two ears and one mouth, meaning I am to listen twice as much as I speak. Actually, one of the best antidotes I have discovered is quiet centering prayer. The more I still my inner voice, as well as my outer voice, and just sit quietly in God's presence each day, the less impulsive my speech becomes. I occasionally think of Gandhi's idea of fasting from speaking, perhaps as often as one day a week, to gain some control over my all too quick tongue. Good communication begins in silence.

Prayer: Jesus, you spoke out of a prayerful spirit. You retreated daily to be silent with your God. You never seemed to be in a rush, like I am most of the time. Slow me down, Jesus. Help me find opportunities for more "being" and less "doing." Help me relax my body, breathe deeply, and soften my gestures and tone of voice. Help me put pauses in my busyness, allowing at least one period of silent aloneness in my daily routine. Quiet my spirit and help me restrain my tongue. Remove my lingering fear of being taken advantage of and help me listen with a receptive, loving heart.

Reflection: How can you build some silent listening to God into your regular routine? How can you help create an environment in your home that encourages better listening?

Songs: "Servant Song" (Donna Marie McGargill); "Sounds of Silence" (Paul Simon); "Come to the Water" (John Foley)

Books: *The Miracle of Mindfulness: A Manual on Meditation* by Thich Nhat Hanh (Boston: Beacon Press, 1996), A; *An Interrupted Life* by Etty Hillesum (New York: Pocket Books, 1991), T/A; *Wherever You Go, There You Are* by Jon Kabat-Zinn (New York: Hyperion, 1994), A
Videos: *Footloose* (a father learns to listen), T/A

3. Kind Words and Soft Answers

A soft answer turns away wrath, / but a harsh word stirs up anger.... / A gentle tongue is a tree of life. (Proverbs 15:1,4)

Fathers, do not provoke [or nag] your children, or they may lose heart. (Colossians 3:21)

The Sufis advise us to speak only after our words have managed to pass through three gates. At the first gate we ask ourselves, "Are these words true?" If so, we let them pass on; if not, back they go. At the second gate we ask, "Are they necessary?" At the last gate we ask, "Are they kind?" (Eknath Eswaren, "Meditation," quoted in *Peacemaking: Day by Day*, Volume 1, page 59)

It was Holy Family Sunday at our church and the Scripture reading began with the words, "Children, obey your parents." I nudged our then ten-year-old son with a gentle elbow and said, "Did you hear that, Tom?" Before Tom had a chance to respond, the lector completed the reading from Colossians with "Fathers, don't nag your children, lest they lose heart." Tom's elbow found my rib cage as his words found my ears: "Dad, did you hear that?"

I did hear and continue to hear those words almost two decades later. Even with our grown children, we still wonder whether we ask too many questions about their future, their commitments, their loan payments, etc. At some point, helpful reminders and questions cross the line and turn into nagging. Nagging shuts down communication and drives adults and children further apart; it has the same effect in the work place.

The Sufi reflection has helped me many times, especially in communicating with my spouse. Even with regard to decisions she has made and wants to follow through on, my "gentle" reminders may not seem so gentle to her. Maybe she isn't doing what she said she would, but must I remind her? Maybe; maybe not. How kind would my words be if I chose to speak? In cases of behavior that is truly self-destructive or hurtful to others, my words may well be true, necessary, and kind. But in other situations, the same words may be closer to nagging.

Parents, teachers, and supervisors all have to "pick their battles." If we challenge others on everything we notice that's wrong, we may become less effective when things really matter. Those we are always challenging may lose heart, perform poorly, tune out, or even drop out.

As we age, Kathy and I realize how forgetful we are becoming. Thus, we've agreed not to get angry at each other over reminders because more often than not, one of us has, in fact, forgotten what we agreed to do. But, again, there are kind reminding words and tones of voice—and not so kind.

Prayer: Patient and kind Abba God, please help us remember our sinfulness. Help us be patient and kind whenever we speak. Jesus, you saw and appealed to the goodness in Matthew and Zacchaeus—both tax collectors—to the goodness in the Samaritan woman at the well, and to the goodness in so many others. Help us see past our own shortcomings and those of others. Help us use kind words to encourage the best in ourselves and others.

Reflection: Are the three criteria for worthwhile speech—true, necessary, and kind—helpful for situations you are in? How can you say helpful things to members in your family or community, using words that don't sound like nagging?

Songs: "Use a Word" (*Teaching Peace*, see page 120); "Father and Son" (Cat Stevens); "You've Got a Friend" (Carol King)

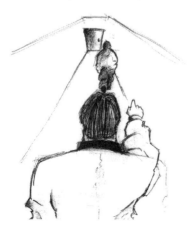

Books: *The Sun and the Wind* by Cornelia Lehn (Newton, KS: Faith and Life Press, 1983), WF; *How To Avoid World War III at Home* by Elizabeth Loescher and Virginia Vobejda (Denver, CO: The Conflict Center, 1994), T/A; *Spinky Sulks* by William Steig (New York: Farrar, 1988), WF

Videos: *Grand Canyon* (good scene of a parent teaching a youth to drive), T/A

4. "I Messages" Break the Cycle of Violence

Keep your tongue from evil, / and your lips from speaking deceit. (Psalm 34:13)

"First take the log out of your own eye, and then you will see clearly to take the speck out of your neighbor's eye." (Matthew 7:5; also Luke 6:42)

We are so quick to judge others, so quick with "you messages." But "you messages" usually escalate a conflict. "You lazy jerk!" "Lazy jerk? Who do you think you are, some kind of almighty judge? All you do around here is complain. You never...." We know exactly how such exchanges take place and how they can escalate into full-blown fights.

"I messages" break this cycle of verbal violence and offer us a "third way" to deal with conflict. Many people know only two ways: fight or flight. Indeed, walking away from a conflictual situation sometimes is prudent. But in many situations it would be better to challenge the injustice or stand up for oneself—without violence.

The best "I messages" have four components: "I feel...when... because...and I want...." For example, "I feel *angry, used, and a little confused* when *you don't do what you say you will*, because *I then end up doing all the tasks and feeling resentful the whole time*. I want *you to follow through on your commitments*." That is so much more productive and respectful than starting with a "you message." If this direct statement doesn't produce the desired results, you can try restating it more forcefully: "I'm not sure I made myself clear. I really do feel resentful when...." If this still doesn't work, try adding a realistic consequence: "I have told you how angry I get when we're having company and you don't do the tasks you agree to do. If we can't share the preparation, I can't agree to having friends over as often." Finally, if this still doesn't work, you can take it to the next level and carry out the consequence.

This kind of verbal assertiveness is a critical skill everyone should learn. It takes practice, of course, but it also requires a different attitude or mindset. It's really a spiritual discipline. I take ownership over my feelings while respecting the dignity of others and refusing to hurt them with my words. I look at my behavior honestly and refrain from judging others and jumping to conclusions. But I don't let myself be violated or victimized. I take a risk to stand up for myself, but I refuse to fight.

Prayer: Jesus, you were careful not to judge others harshly. There were times when you walked away from those wanting to harm you, like those in Nazareth who wanted to kill you because they thought you were claiming to be God. But there were other times when you defended yourself. You told Peter to put away his sword when they came for you in the Garden of Gethsemane. You resisted, not with weapons, but with your words. Help me develop the courage and skill to resist respectfully.

Reflection: What situations offer you the opportunity to use the four-phased "I message" as a good alternative to fight or flight? How can you encourage members in your family to use "I messages" and to be more verbally asserted when it is appropriate?

Songs: "We Can Work It Out" (Beatles); "They'll Know We Are Christians" (Peter Scholtes)
Books: *Angel Child, Dragon Child* by Michele Maria Surat (New York: Scholastic Inc., 1989; Vietnamese girls tell their story to

taunting classmates), WF; *A Volcano in My Tummy: Helping Children to Handle Anger* by Elaine Whitehouse and Warwick Pudney (Santa Cruz, CA: New Society Publishers, 1996), WF
Videos: *Do the Right Thing* (how not to deal with differences), T/A

5. Dampen Anger with "Cold Water Words"

"But I say to you, Love your enemies." (Matthew 5:44)

The Lord GOD has given me the tongue of a teacher, / that I may know how to sustain the weary with a word. / Morning by morning God wakens... / my ear to listen. (Isaiah 50:4)

Often in anger, and especially when we are weary, we say things that we regret. Feeling hurt or attacked, we counter-attack with words and gestures that only fuel the flames of discord and escalate the negative situation. Although it takes some self-control, there are words and ways to defuse or de-escalate a conflict. Some practitioners of anger management call these "cold water words." More and more I am learning how helpful these "cold water words" can be. For example, I can remember an exchange with one of our sons when he was a teenager. We were in the midst of an argument, face to face, fists clenched, when I said, "We can do better than this." I didn't say *"You* can do better than this." Rather, I took responsibility for my own part in the conflict and appealed to the best in both of us.

There are many such examples. A friend told me that he has used the expression "Let's not go down that road" in a number of conflicts at work. "Maybe you're right" or "Let's start over" also are ways to stop battles before they get out of hand, to remind ourselves that we can indeed do it differently. All these expressions have a way of cutting the emotional tension and the physical rush of adrenaline that are part of an escalating argument.

The inner attitude that nurtures these outward conciliatory expressions is reflected in the two Scripture passages above. First, we can take Jesus' words a step further. When Jesus says "Love your enemies," we can refuse to think of those with whom we are in conflict as "enemies" in the first place. We can choose to see the other person as a child of God, like ourselves; loved by God, like ourselves. We can think of how the other person may be just as fearful, if not more so, than we are in the situation.

We also can develop this inner attitude of respect for all persons by praying each day for this gift and by listening to God's consoling words. If we start the day by placing ourselves in the presence of God's love, we are more likely to be instruments of that love throughout the day. Consoled by God, we can speak consoling, defusing words to others.

Prayer: Jesus, I have lost control at times and heaped verbal coals of fire on others—even those I love the most. Please forgive me. Help me to see the hurts and fears in others and to let go of my own. Help me to stay centered, even in the midst of conflict, and to use a vocabulary of love and conciliation.

Reflection: What "cold water words" might work for you? What else can you do in your family to keep arguments from turning into fights?

Songs: "All You Need Is Love" (Beatles); "Peace Prayer of Saint Francis" (John Foley)
Books: *Mean Soup* by B. Everitt (New York: Harcourt, Brace, 1992; a mother pulls her angry son out of his meanness with "mean soup"), WF; *Fighting Fair for Families* by Fran Schmidt and Alice Friedman (Miami, FL: Peace Works, 1989), T/A
Videos: *Baghdad Cafe* (a stranger heals an angry woman), T/A

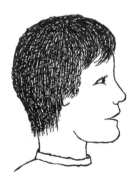

27

6. Giving God the Anger
Nancy Hastings Sehested

Be angry but do not sin; do not let the sun go down on your anger. (Ephesians 4:26)

Rash words are like sword thrusts, / but the tongue of the wise brings healing. (Proverbs 12:18)

One Sunday I called a church member and asked him to read a psalm in the worship service. Later, he called me back to say I had mistakenly given him Psalm 109. When I told him that was the correct psalm, he was appalled. "But it isn't nice!" he insisted. "I can't read something so angry in the worship service." And he was right; Psalm 109 is not nice. But then, we are not nice at times, especially when we are angry.

Have you ever been angry with someone—your spouse or children, for instance, for forgetting your birthday? Have you been mad at your parents because they were unreasonable about curfew? Perhaps it was something much worse. Have you been the victim of a crime, or has a friend betrayed you? Did your parents divorce or did a drunk driver kill someone you love? Maybe life in general simply has not turned out the way you wanted. There are countless good reasons to be angry. What do you do with your anger?

The Bible is honest about anger. Many psalms, for example, speak about the urge for vengeance when we have been wronged. One of them is Psalm 109. The wounded psalmist is hopping mad because lies are being said about him, there is not a thing he has done to deserve this treatment, and God seems to be silent about it all. The psalmist asks God to pay attention and to take a good look at the unfair situation. It's as if the psalmist is saying, "God, if you need some ideas about what to do with this creep, let me give you a few." Then the list of suggestions for vengeance begins: "May his days be few...may someone seize his goods...may no one be kind to him." The rage goes on and on.

Finally, spent of all rage, the psalmist realizes that there are not enough ways to hurt his enemy to set things right. In verse 22, the prayer turns to the wounded heart of the psalmist: "For I am poor and needy, / and my heart is pierced within me."

If you have had an enemy, you've probably wanted vengeance. But vengeance is not in our hands. Our anger is not to be acted upon; our anger is to be offered to God. Anger is good in that it acts like a fever that burns the toxins out of our bodies so that we can be healed. But none of us can live forever in a fevered state. Sustained anger burns down our own house while leaving casualties all around. In the end, it is only God who can heal so deep a wound. The anger within us is released and the enemy is released into the hands of a transforming God. Healing is then possible.

Prayer: O God, we offer to you the angers and resentments that we hold close. Touch our deeply wounded heart with your healing hand.

Reflection: Is there an injustice or hurt that has happened to you that still makes you angry? Could you turn it over to God? What happens when members of your family are angry at one another? How can you learn together to release "family anger" to God?

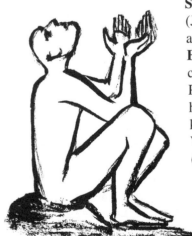

Songs: "Heaven on Their Mind" (Jesus Christ Superstar); "Fire and Rain" (James Taylor)
Books: *I Was So Angry* by Mercer Mayer (Racine, WI: Western Publishing, 1983; a mother heals her child's rage with an act of kindness), WF
Videos: *The Great Santini* (when his abusive father dies, Ben fears that it is his anger that contributed to his father's death), T/A

LET GO OF THE ANGER

7. Gratitude Makes Peace

One given to anger stirs up strife. (Proverbs 29:22)

And let the peace of Christ rule in your hearts, to which indeed you were called in the one body. And be thankful....And whatever you do, in word or deed, do everything in the name of the Lord Jesus, giving thanks to God. (Colossians 3:15,17)

The last years of life for Kathy's mother were difficult. Senility impeded both her memory and her attempts to communicate. In the face of diminished capacity and increased discomfort, however, Rosemary's core spirit remained to the end. Her simple words of gratitude and her smiles transformed her final weeks. Her nursing home aides seemed to become more caring and often told us that she was a wonderful person. Although she didn't know who any of us were, Rosemary always said, "Thank you for coming to visit."

We wondered why God let Rosemary linger so long. Perhaps it was to give us the opportunity to become more caring persons and to learn the value of a simple, gentle, grateful spirit. Through it all we did, indeed, learn a powerful lesson: While anger stirs up strife, gratitude makes peace.

A gentle, grateful, spirit can change the dynamics of an entire group, whether it is a family, a work place, a classroom, a committee meeting, or a social gathering. We can develop a grateful spirit by regularly reflecting on the fact that all we are and have is gift. Then in gratitude to God and all who nurture us, we can try to respond positively to each person and situation we encounter. We can notice, affirm, and remember the best in others and the positive potential in any situation we are in.

This takes discipline, of course. It is often easier to catch people doing wrong than to catch them doing good. We simply have to remind ourselves to notice and affirm each positive deed we see, and to consider these kindnesses and deeds as gifts. We can say "Thanks," no matter how small or ordinary an act may seem to be.

The grateful person uplifts individuals and groups. The grateful person attracts others. The grateful person's goodness is contagious. The grateful person is a bearer of the peace of Christ to his or her family, faith community, and the world.

Individually, we can start this process with thoughts and words of thanks: thanks to God, thanks for Jesus, thanks for life and all the gifts of creation. Thanks for our own individual giftedness and the giftedness of each person in our lives. One creative way of reinforcing gratitude is to keep a "blessing book" in which we write down the blessings, gifts, and goodness of each day. A grateful heart can't be a hateful heart.

Prayer: Thank you, lavish God, for all you have given me. Thank you for the example of the simple, gentle, grateful persons in my life. Help me to walk in gratitude with the words "Thank you" ever on my lips. "May the words of my mouth and the meditation of my heart be acceptable to you, O God."

Reflection: Reflect on all the gifts you are and have and all the situations God has placed you in. How can you be more of a grateful, peaceful presence in those situations? What are some of the little gifts you have received from other family members? What can your family do to remember to say "Thank you" more often?

Songs: "God Is So Good" (traditional); "Now Thank We All Our God" (Martin Rinkart); "All My Days" (Dan Schutte)
Books: *The Worst Person in the World* by James Stevenson, (New York: Morrow Co., 1995; kids' kindnesses help a "grouch" become grateful), WF
Videos: *Matewan* (a union organizer unifies groups of miners), T/A

Mahalo   *Merci*

GRACIAS

Grazie   **Danke**

Part III
Listen Carefully

To listen carefully to others, especially those who disagree with me, and to consider others' feelings and needs rather than insist on having my own way

1. Prayerful and Careful Listening

I will now allure her, / and bring her into the wilderness, / and speak tenderly to her. (Hosea 2:14)

"Be still and know that I am God." (Psalm 46:10)

W hen I told my spiritual director that I was not a good listener, he gave me the following prescription: "Try centering prayer twice a day for ten minutes." When I looked a little puzzled, he said, "Find a quiet place, sit upright with your hands in your lap and palms up and barely touching each other, and place yourself in silent surrender before God. Select a mantra like 'Be still and know that I am God' and say it whenever you begin to be distracted. Attune yourself to God and just be." Basil Pennington describes centering prayer in this way: God is always sending out signals. Like radio waves, those signals are invisible. To hear them, we must turn on the "receiver" by becoming still and silent.

Early morning, after work, and sometimes late at night when everyone is in bed are my most attentive times. Once I found the best times and places, I discovered that ten minutes wasn't very long. In fact, over the years the ten minutes lengthened as God lured me to my places of prayer at home and on the road. I began to trust that this truly was not "wasted time," even when I would start daydreaming or falling asleep. With time, I found that the more willing I was to just sit there, be aware of the divine Spirit within, and listen for God's promptings, the more willing I became to sit and listen to others.

Not every prayer time has to be filled with insight, of course. Likewise, not every conversation has to seem significant to be worthwhile. If there is time in our day to spend on prayerful listening to God, there probably will be, not surprisingly, a little more time for careful listening to people. Then, little by little, we become that "non-anxious presence" that counselors say is so important for calming tense or conflictual situations.

Like Hosea, many people find themselves especially attentive to God when lured by God into wilderness places like the desert, on a mountain top, beside a country stream, or in a flowering meadow. God can be so tangibly present in these places of dramatic natural beauty that we need these experiences to supplement our regular prayer places. Our Creator truly does lure us into creation, into that Garden of Eden where God wants to walk with us hand in hand. Attentive silence before the Spirit who breathed creation into being enhances our attentiveness to all around us.

A centered self is not self-centered; rather, a centered self is tuned outward as well as inward. To become good listeners we need to heed this upside-down insight: "Don't just do something, sit there!"

Prayer: Sabbath God, free me from the mistaken notion that I need to fill every empty space in my life with doing. Teach me how to be, to balance doing with being. Alluring God, lure me into places of beauty and silence so that I can learn to listen prayerfully to you and then listen carefully to the people you place in my life this day, this week.

Reflection: How can you build prayerful listening into each day—at home and on the road? How can you encourage members of your family to listen more prayerfully to God?

Songs: "El Shadai" (Michael Card); "Sounds of Silence" (Paul Simon); "Hush, Hush, Somebody's Callin' Mah Name" (African-American spiritual)
Books: *The Little Prince* by Antoine de Saint-Exupery (New York: Harcourt, Brace and World, 1943), WF
Videos: *Tea House of the August Moon* (an Army captain learns how to "center" through the Japanese tea ceremony), T/A

2. Listening for Needs

"Zacchaeus, hurry and come down; for I must stay at your house today." (Luke 19:5)

You shall love your neighbor as yourself. (Leviticus 19:18; Mark 12:31)

O ther-centeredness begins with listening, and listening is an integral part of loving. Listening enables us to tune in to the needs of others. Good listeners have their antennas out, listening for clues from others about what they need. Listening carefully enables us to know what questions to ask, what words to say, what resources to suggest—and when to keep quiet.

Jesus was such a listener. His antennas were highly sensitive. He could tell what people needed, when crowds were distressed, when individuals were hurting. He was able to address these needs because he listened. People felt understood in his presence—and as a result, they often made major changes in their lives. This seems true of Mary Magdalene and Zacchaeus. Jesus must have listened well during that dinner with Zacchaeus' family because when Jesus left, Zacchaeus was a new person.

Children didn't need to misbehave to get Jesus' attention; he welcomed children and listened to them. He even chided his disciples for trying to protect his time for more important people.

Dorothy Day was like that. She could sit in one of her Catholic Worker houses and listen for hours to less than fully coherent elderly people, because she considered them "ambassadors of God." "Once they are taken in," she said, "they become members of the family." Like Mother Teresa, Dorothy Day saw the face of Christ in each person.

Listening enables us to act more appropriately, helpfully, and surprisingly. One of the loving outcomes of careful listening is being able to identify little surprises or gifts that will please those dear to us. Careful listeners have no problem selecting or making gifts. Generous listeners know when to bring flowers, help with— or even do—another person's chores, write notes, serve breakfast in bed, or any number of other random acts of kindness. Good listeners are great lovers.

No one is unworthy of our attentiveness—and that includes ourselves. Francis of Assisi understood obedience as listening to the will of God, to the needs of others, and to our own needs. "Love your neighbor as yourself" means listening to ourselves as well as listening to others. To be compassionate toward ourselves means listening to and responding to our own needs—for rest, for relief, for creativity, for companionship, for prayer, for time away, for time alone. If we aren't getting our own needs met, we aren't much good for others. This kind of listening, of course, often requires a sounding board—a soul brother or sister, a spouse, a spiritual director, a counselor, a close relative, or all of the above.

Prayer: Jesus, help me to be the kind of listener you were and still are. Help me keep from becoming so busy that I can't find time to be present to others—as well as to my own needs. Help me to be a great listener so that I can truly be a good lover.

Reflection: What is the main obstacle that keeps you from fully tuning in to the needs of others? What can you do to overcome this obstacle? How can your family members become more attuned to one another?

Songs: "Slow Down" (Chuck Girard); "Listen to the Lambs" (R. Nathaniel Dett; African-American)
Books: *Grandmama's Joy* by Eloise Greenfield (New York: Philomel Books, 1980), WF; *Love Is the Measure* by Jim Forest (Maryknoll, NY: Orbis Books, 1994, a biography of Dorothy Day), T/A
Videos: *Entertaining Angels* (a woman's suicide teaches Dorothy Day the importance of listening), T/A

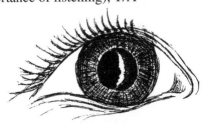

3. Listening with Your Whole Self

Palmira Perea-Hay

Some people keep silent because they have nothing to say, /
while others keep silent because they know when to speak. /
The wise remain silent until the right moment. (Sirach 20:6-7)

There are many Scriptures that come to my mind as I meditate on "listening." Among them are these words from Sirach about keeping quiet until the time is right. How are we to know, though, when the right time is right? Only by listening! That is a circumventing answer, you might say.

I had the privilege of living for nearly eighteen years with my sister who was deaf. I lived with her twelve more years after she lost her sight as well. During that time, I learned many lessons from her about patience, trust, faith, and the importance of listening.

For example, we frequently talk about learning to listen with our eyes as well as with our ears. When neither our eyes nor our ears work for us, however, we are challenged to listen with our heart. I learned that from my sister. Communication is deeper than words exchanged; it is an exchange of the deepest part of ourselves—our feelings, our aspirations, and our desires. When I communicated with my sister through tactile American sign language, I had to put my entire self at her service, as she did with me. When communicating with a deaf-blind person, we cannot look around or have the TV on because we have to watch the sign language and the expressions on the face of the person.

I often wonder why we don't use that same skill when we communicate with a person who has sight and can speak. Is it because we give in to all other distractions? Is it because we might be tapped for more than we want to give at the time? Is it a matter of not wanting to really be present to the other? Is it a matter of wanting to be present to everybody at the expense of not giving our attention to the person in front of us?

To listen, to be fully present, is the greatest gift we can give another. When I have someone's undivided attention, I feel important; I feel valued; I feel like I want to be for others in that same way.

Wisdom comes from the recesses of our souls, so when we truly listen to others, we share that wisdom that comes from God.

Prayer: Help me, O God, to listen to you so that I might be ready to listen to those with whom I will interact today. Help me focus my whole self on others and give them my undivided attention and love. Help me remember that each encounter is an opportunity to meet you and to bring you to the people in my day.

Reflection: Recall the last time you were at the center of another's attention, when the other was really listening to you. What were your feelings? Would a listening exercise be helpful and fun in your family? For example, consider taking turns listening to one another for two or three minutes and then providing feedback, repeating as precisely as possible what was heard. Then discuss what you learned from the exercise and how you could put it into practice on a regular basis.

Songs: "If You Hear the Voice of God: Psalm 95" (MacAller); "Seek the Lord" (Roc O'Connor)

Books: *Grandpa's Face* by Eloise Greenfield (New York: Philomel Books, 1988), WF; *How to Talk So Kids Will Listen and Listen So Kids Will Talk* by Adele Faber and Elaine Mazlish (New York: Avon Books, 1982), T/A

Videos: *Ordinary People* (a suicidal teen finds a model listener in his therapist), T/A

4. Listening as Hospitality

"Martha, Martha, you are worried and distracted by many things; there is need of only one thing. Mary has chosen the better part." (Luke 10:41,42)

Teach this triple truth to all: A generous heart, kind speech, and a life of service and compassion are the things which renew humanity. (Buddha, quoted in *Peacemaking: Day by Day*, Volume 2, page 36)

"Let me bring a little bread, that you may refresh yourselves, and after that you may pass on, since you have come to your servant [Abraham]." (Genesis 18:5)

We often get so busy with our inflexible schedules that we can't hear what others are saying, and we miss opportunities for enrichment. Jesus says that Mary, not Martha, has chosen the better part because Mary is fully present to her guests.

We never know when Jesus (in the person of others) may be present. Every meeting is pregnant with possibility. If we make ourselves fully available, who knows where it might lead, who we might meet, what good we might be able to do. Mary sits at the feet of her guest, listens, and is blessed by the Master. Our Master is always there, disguised. It's the receptive, listening person who can see through the disguise, discover the gift, and come away enriched.

Some people seem to have the ability to be present to others no matter what. It's not an innate ability, however; it's a chosen way of being, the fruit of deciding over and over that people are more important than tasks. We can always get back to the task, but we may not get another opportunity to be present to our child, our spouse, or this caller.

Jesus is the model listener. He's a frequent dinner guest, loves weddings, and always has time for people, especially children and those who are hurting. Granted, he doesn't have a nine-to-five job, kids to drive everywhere, shopping to do, committees to serve on. But, as the wonderful *Joshua* stories reveal, if he had these responsibilities, he would see all as opportunities to tune in to those around him. He has a hospitable heart, like Mary.

But we also have to honor Martha. She is being hospitable by making the environment comfortable and the food delicious for her guests. But it isn't her dedication to service that Jesus criticizes; it's her uncentered preoccupation with the tasks themselves.

How often we get frantic with everything that needs to be done when company is coming. We get short-tempered and forget the real purpose behind the event—loving service of others. The remedy to this frantic activity and poor disposition lies in sharing the preparation tasks and starting early. In a family or community situation, all members can share in preparing for the feast so that all can share in the hospitality of listening and fellowship that follows the feast.

Prayer: Jesus, you are always, ultimately, the guest, the visitor, the caller. Remind us to drop what we are doing that we might listen to your voice in others and respond. Help us keep close to you throughout our day, ready to meet you when you call. Help us to use the routine events of our day as opportunities to be present to others and to add loving touches to our tasks of service.

Reflection: What can you do to become more attentive to others? What can you do as a family or community to be less harried, and more attentive, and to make your home more available to others?

Songs: "God Has Chosen Me" (Bernadette Farrell); "Turn to Me" (John Foley)

Books: *Joshua* and *Joshua and the Children* by Joseph F. Girzone (New York: Simon & Schuster, 1995), WF

Videos: *Mr. Holland's Opus* (a musician becomes an attentive teacher), T/A; *Entertaining Angels* (the story of Dorothy Day's houses of hospitality), T/A

5. Listening as Yielding

"The greatest among you must become like the youngest, and the leader like one who serves." (Luke 22:26)

"Abba, Father…remove this cup from me; yet, not what I want, but what you want." (Mark 14:36)

Through love become slaves to one another. (Galatians 5:13)

"Someone else will fasten a belt around you and take you where you do not wish to go." (John 21:18)

Much of the violence within our hearts and in our society comes from a desire to be in charge, to be first, to win. We want to be first in line whenever there is food, a sale, or a ticket to buy. Some of us are always passing others on the highway to get to our exit as fast as we can, rather than falling back behind others in the exit lane. In conversations we want to be in control, get in all we want to say, and make sure the outcome is what we planned. It's not just men who want to be in charge, but most of us men do seem to have this desire. Frankly, we like being on top. We tend to dominate.

Listening is a powerful antidote to this desire to dominate. When we listen carefully, we let go of our own agenda and focus on others. We do not hurriedly craft our response in order to win a point; rather, we try to understand what others are saying and to sense how they are feeling.

Careful listeners are "active listeners." Before responding with their own opinion or story, careful listeners feedback or paraphrase what they sense others are feeling and saying. They know that not every verbal encounter needs to be a debate, and not every jaunt down the highway needs to be a race for the exit.

Yielding to others is difficult for people who are bent on winning and controlling. But nonviolence is precisely about yielding control and power. It's not yielding our dignity and letting others abuse or violate us. Rather, it's the yielding of the need to always be in charge. For white social activists, males especially, this involves letting go of the need to be the leader of efforts to overcome injustice. White people, for example, can be allies for people of color in campaigns against racism; people without disabilities can follow the lead of those with disabilities in efforts to make facilities more accessible; men can support women in the struggle against sexism; heterosexual persons can stand with gays and lesbians in challenging discriminatory practices and laws.

Prayer: Jesus, you listened to God and learned to subordinate your will to God's, even at that terrible moment of agony in the Garden of Gethsemane. You taught your disciples to seek the lowest places and to become the servants of others. You warned them that they would be led places where they wouldn't want to go. Help us, Jesus, to let go of that powerful desire to be first, to be in charge. Help us learn to yield to others. Your apostle Paul instructed spouses to defer to each other. May we learn to do so in all our relationships.

Reflection: In what situations do you find yourself wanting to be in charge and/or win? How can you begin to yield to others in those situations? When has leadership or control been taken over and shared by different members of your family or community? How can you increase this sharing of leadership?

Songs: "Teach Your Children" (Graham Nash); "I Only Want to Say" (Superstar)
Books: *How the Grinch Stole Christmas* by Dr. Seuss (New York: Random House, 1957), WF
Videos: *Grand Canyon* (a gentle respectful talk prevents a mugging—or worse), T/A

6. Listening to Our Ancestors
Ken Lovingood

"Some [seed] fell into good soil, and when it grew, it produced a hundredfold." As he said this, he called out, "Let anyone with ears to hear listen!" (Luke 8:8)

We African-Americans have a strong spiritual bond with our ancestors. We believe that we are where we are largely because our ancestors persevered through many hardships. Well documented and still coming to light are the things our ancestors endured to give their children and grandchildren the strength to cope with life. Today, we look to them for continued strength and purpose.

Our ancestors offer to us today the powers that God gave them. There is a ritual, using a pitcher of water and a bowl, that honors and invokes these spiritual powers. The water, which represents life, is poured from the pitcher into the bowl as the names of our ancestors are spoken. At the same time, we name the gifts that each ancestor had and ask that these gifts be passed on to us and strengthened within us. As in the parable of the sower, we pray that the seed falls on good soil and yields a good harvest.

This ritual, a powerful form of listening, affects us deeply. This kind of spiritual listening is active, not passive. That's why the invocation of our ancestors is so important.

In addition to this ritual, there are other ways to listen to the wisdom of our ancestors. Telling our stories, for example, can be very important, or we can ask older family members about the lives of our grandparents and great grandparents—what they did, how they lived. Family photo albums, journals, and boxes of family mementos also can help keep the story alive. We need to learn as much as we can about our own family's history—and we need to preserve this history for those who come after us.

But we need to listen to more than just the wisdom of our own family members; we need to listen to the wisdom of all our people. So we read stories to our children about the struggles of our people, from the time of slavery through the civil rights movement. Popular movies and the "Eyes on the Prize" documentary series on PBS are visually engaging. When we travel, we look for opportunities to visit sites such as the Civil Rights Museum in Memphis and those places in Birmingham and elsewhere in the South where our people struggled for justice. The museum of the Negro Baseball Leagues in Kansas City is an engaging experience for all ages. African-American art galleries and museums also keep our story and wisdom available for those who have eyes and ears willing to see, listen, and learn.

Prayer: Dear Lord, help us to listen to others. Give us the strength to go beyond our fears and attitudes. Give us the wisdom to allow what others say and do to affect us positively. Touch us with the wisdom of those who have gone before us in faith and good will.

Reflection: What can you do to learn more about the traditions of your family and your cultural history? How are you keeping your family and cultural stories alive in your family?

Songs: "We've Come This Far by Faith" (Albert Goodson); "Deep River" (traditional spiritual); "Day Is Done" (Peter Yarrow)
Books: *Pass It On: African-American Poetry for Children* selected by Wade Hudson (New York: Scholastic, 1993), WF; *Mirandy and Brother Wind* by Patricia McKissack (New York: Knopf, 1988), WF; *American Indian Myths and Legends* by Richard Erdoes and Alfonso Ortiz (New York: Pantheon Books, 1985), T/A
Videos: "Eyes on the Prize" (PBS series), T/A; *Long Walk Home* (a fictional account of the Montgomery bus boycott), WF; *I Know Why the Caged Bird Sings* (Maya Angelou's story of growing up in a segregated society), T/A; *Amistad* (the historical retelling of slaves revolting, demanding their freedom), T/A

7. "No More Meanness"

Nancy Hastings Sehested

Be kind to one another, tenderhearted, forgiving one another, as God in Christ has forgiven you. (Ephesians 4:32)

It was parent night at the end of our week of Vacation Bible School at the Sweet Fellowship Baptist Church. After much practice, each child's group was prepared to act out for the parents a dramatic presentation of a Bible story. One group consisted of four lively five-year-old boys prepared to act out the story of Moses and the Hebrew slaves leaving Egypt. Wielding their plastic swords, the boys especially liked playing the mean Pharaoh and his army who would not let the people go.

At the appropriate time, I nudged our Moses to stand before Pharaoh and say, "Pharaoh, the slaves are all tired and they don't want you bossing them around anymore. Let the people go!" Pharaoh, sitting on his throne and twirling his plastic sword, responded—with prompting—"Never, never, never!"

Young Moses then left the room only to return within seconds. Once again, he approached Pharaoh: "Pharaoh, my people are really tired of being beat up. Now will you let the people go?" Once again, I whispered into our little Pharaoh's ear: "Say 'Never, never, never,' " but Pharaoh had had enough. He jumped down from his throne and said, "I don't want to be mean anymore. All of you can go! Just go! You can all go home now." Then he threw his sword on the floor and walked off with his arm draped around Moses.

Could it be true? Can the story be reimagined in our day? Can Pharaoh's heart be draped with mercy? Is it possible that the mean people of the world will grow tired of being mean? What would it take to bring that about?

One of the first steps would be active listening. In the biblical story, Pharaoh had no desire to listen to anyone; he insisted on having his own way. Hearing about all the hurts and struggles of the Hebrew people did not matter to him. He was determined to have his way even if it harmed other people.

God saw how hard Moses worked to get Pharaoh to pay attention, but Pharaoh's heart was hardened; there was no hope for peaceful negotiations. As a result, Moses had to let go of Pharaoh to get on with his task of leading the people to a land of freedom. This story is a tragic reminder of the consequences of not listening.

Our five-year-old Pharaoh listened and truly heard Moses' cries on behalf of those who suffered. He heard with his heart and laid down his sword of meanness. He even let go of insisting on having his own way. His listening heart transformed an enemy into a friend.

Has the world grown tired of being mean? Can we listen with our hearts and be at peace?

Prayer: Listening God, teach us to listen with hearts of love and understanding. May we all grow tired of being mean to each other so that we can live in peace.

Reflection: Can you think of a time when you were not heard by someone who disagreed with you? Were you able to hear that person's point of view? Can you remember a time when you were enemies with someone, and you were mean to each other? Did the situation ever change by listening to each other's feelings?

Songs: "Two Hangmen" (Mason Prophet; John Michael Talbot); "We Can Work It Out" (Beatles)

Books: *Katie, Kit and Cousin Tom* by Tomie DePaola (New York: Simon and Schuster, 1986; a "mean" boy learns to be cooperative), WF

Videos: *Kramer vs. Kramer* (a neglectful husband/father learns to listen), T/A

Part IV
Forgive

To apologize and make amends when I have hurt another,
to forgive others, and to keep from holding grudges

1. Forgiven and Empowered

When...the doors of the house where the disciples had met were locked for fear..., Jesus came and stood among them and said, "Peace be with you." (John 20:19)

The Lord bless you and keep you...and be gracious to you...and give you peace. (Numbers 6:24,25,26)

The first step toward loving service of others is to accept the forgiveness of God and to accept and forgive ourselves. Only then are we free from a paralyzing guilt that keeps us self-centered and unable to focus on others. We violate our own dignity and fail to respect ourselves when we refuse to forgive ourselves and accept God's forgiveness.

What a forgiving God we have. What an accepting and empowering Lord we follow. Jesus knew that, except for John, all his disciples had all deserted him. He knew of Peter's denials and of his disciples' fear of experiencing his same fate. He knew they huddled behind locked doors.

But Jesus did not chide his disciples. Rather, he spoke words of acceptance and peace. When he appeared in their midst that Easter Sunday evening, his first words were "Peace be with you." He met and accepted his disciples right where they were, with all their fears and failings. But in this act of forgiving acceptance, he empowered them to go forth. "As the Father has sent me, so I send you." He gave them what they needed for their mission of self-sacrificing service. "Receive the Holy Spirit." These same fearful followers would become fearless and faithful instruments of God's transforming love.

This same accepting, forgiving, empowering Jesus calls us each day in a similar way. In prayerful silence or in the celebration of the Eucharist or Lord's Supper, we hear these same words: "Peace be with you." In some faith traditions, people have access to a "sacrament" or "rite" of reconciliation, in which they experience these same forgiving words, this same liberating grace.

Families can also be places where forgiveness is sought and

received. Contrite adults and children can acknowledge their hurtful words and deeds, ask forgiveness, make amends, and be forgiven. This experience, often sealed with tender touches or hugs, can be a healing balm that binds family members back together, extends their sense of trust and security, and sends them forth to be instruments of God's forgiving love in the world.

Prayer: Jesus, slow us down so we can hear your words of peace and feel your forgiving love. We have not been all that you called us to be. We have failed and fallen—often. You fell, too, under the weight of your cross. But each time you got back up and struggled on. Help us to start anew after each fall. Give us the humility and courage to ask forgiveness of those we have hurt and to extend forgiveness to those who have hurt us. Let us break the cycle of violence with acts of contrition and forgiveness.

Reflection: What is keeping you from feeling God's forgiving love? How can you create an atmosphere of acceptance that encourages acts of apology, amendment, and forgiveness at home or in other intimate circles?

Songs: "Peace I Leave with You, My Friends" (Ray Repp); "Cristo Es Nuestra Paz" (*Jubilee*, see page 120); "Where Charity and Love Prevail" (Paul Benoit); "Peace Prayer" (John Foley); "O Happy Day" (Edwin R. Hawkins; African-American spiritual)
Books: *The Hurt* by Teddi Doleski (Mahwah, NJ: Paulist Press, 1983), WF; *Seventy Times Seven* by Johann Arnold (Farmington, PA: Plough Publishing House, 1997), A; *Terry: My Daughter's Life and Death Struggle with Alcoholism* by George McGovern (New York: Random House, 1996), A

Videos: *Places in the Heart* (a wife finds forgiveness for her adulterous husband during a Communion service), T/A

51

2. "Cold Water Deeds" Can Put Out Fires

"If anyone forces you to go one mile, go also the second mile." (Matthew 5:41; Romans 12:20)

If your enemies are hungry, give them bread to eat... / for you will heap coals of fire on their heads. (Proverbs 25:21,22)

It is the servants of the all-merciful Lord who go about the earth in modesty and who answer "peace" when accosted by those who talk to them rudely. (Qur'an, quoted in *Peace Prayers*, San Francisco: Harper, 1992; page 122)

Just as there are "cold water words" that can put out disputes before they turn into raging infernos, there are "cold water deeds" that can break the cycle of violence and head a relationship back in the right direction. These are practical applications of Jesus' command to love our enemies and do good to those who persecute us.

Well, they weren't really my enemies and they weren't exactly persecuting me, but I did feel taken advantage of and I didn't feel especially friendly that Easter Monday years ago. During Holy Week I hid a stick of my favorite salami in the refrigerator to enjoy after Easter. Easter Monday, when I discovered it was gone, I was furious. Storming around, I threatened dire consequences if the culprit didn't come forth. No one admitted blame.

I decided to try a different approach. The next evening, I bought another salami and declared a "happy hour," inviting the whole family to enjoy the treat. I'm not sure about the impact of that initiative, but it did transform my heart a little.

The Qur'an suggests that we respond to rude words with words of peace. It sounds easier than it is, but it is what the children of an all-merciful God do. They respond to a mean or frowning face with a smile.

On the level of social issues, the story of six-year-old Ruby Bridges (see page 110) shows the power of loving and forgiving initiatives. Her prayers for her tormenters helped keep that violent situation from becoming even more violent. On a broader scale, Nelson Mandela's kindnesses toward his South African jailers during his twenty-seven-year imprisonment were reciprocated. And Mandela's willingness and courage to forgive and work with his racist opponents helped heal a nation steeped in violence.

Jesus does not guarantee that others will stop taking advantage of us if we carry their load an extra mile. But he does say that such a response will make them think. Maybe they will see the error of their ways and repent—maybe not. Or maybe not immediately but at a later date. Our actions will have contributed to the final outcome.

Such courageous initiatives help heal our broken world, for even when our actions don't convert others, they do convert us—the doers. Having made one such response to a provocation, we are more likely to do it again, perhaps with more creativity and/or forgiveness.

Prayer: Jesus, help us see that you have called us to be, like you, an instrument of forgiving love. You make it clear that people will do to us exactly what they did to you. You do not take us out of the world, but you give us your Spirit of courageous love. Spirit of forgiving love, melt us, mold us, fill us, use us. Spirit of forgiving love, fall afresh on us.

Reflection: Is there a situation or a relationship in your life that might be healed or can begin to heal by a unilateral act of forgiving love? How can you foster this value of forgiving love in your family or community?

Songs: "Spirit of the Living God" (Daniel Iverson)

Books: *Here Comes the Cat!* by Vladimir Vagin and Frank Asch (New York: Scholastic Books, 1989), WF; *The Forgiveness Factor: Stories of Hope in a World of Conflict* by Michael Henderson (Salem, OR: Grosvenor Books, 1996), T/A

Videos: *Karate Kid II* (loving one's enemies), WF; *Les Miserables* (forgiveness heals), A

3. A "Forgiveness Party"

"But while he was still far off, his father saw him and was filled with compassion; he ran and put his arms around him and kissed him." (Luke 15:20)

When slandered, we speak kindly. (1 Corinthians 4:13)

But if a person forgives and makes reconciliation, their reward is due from Allah. (Qur'an 42:40)

The process of reconciliation generally goes through at least three stages: remorse, restitution, and reconciliation. The parable of the prodigal son illustrates these stages. The prodigal son discovers the error of his ways and remorsefully returns to his father, asking only to be a hired hand. The father readily forgives his son and throws a feast as his way of completing the process of reconciliation.

A recent variation of this "forgiveness party" was printed in *Fellowship* magazine. Nine-year-old Bess discovered her room had been burglarized, costing her a new "boom box," $17 in allowance money, and lots of Valentine's Day candy. She and her mother were sure that the culprits were the same three youths who had defaced their home with hateful graffiti and eggs only weeks earlier. But rather than have the youths arrested, they arranged a meeting with them, their parents, and a police officer. The boys admitted their deeds and agreed to make restitution. They also repainted the house.

But Bess wasn't satisfied with restitution. Something was missing. She realized that she wanted to do something to improve the relationships among the families. She decided to throw a "forgiveness party," complete with music, dancing, food, and a piñata. All three offenders and their families came, and things were never the same in the neighborhood.

I have experienced the power of reconciling actions of another kind. For several years, on the anniversary of the bombing of Hiroshima (August 6) in 1945, I have made an origami paper crane for someone I needed to be reconciled with. These paper cranes became a symbol of peacemaking when eleven-year-old Sadako Sasaki tried to make one thousand of them as she was dying of leukemia contracted as a result of the radiation from the atomic bomb; she made 644 before she died. On the wings of her last paper crane she wrote the word "peace" in Japanese and told the crane to fly over the whole world. Within a few years, children all over the world were making cranes as symbols of peace. I learned to make them from my daughter and have taught thousands of others to make them as symbols of reconciliation. You might write the name of a person on one wing and "peace" on the other and send it with a letter to that person you want to be reconciled with. The person's response is irrelevant; we, at least, have faced up to our own sinfulness, offered our apology, and reached out to the other. We are not in the same place we were before.

Prayer: Jesus, how willing you are to forgive. You welcome sinners into your heart and enable them to find remorse. You do this for me, over and over again. Help me find the courage to do this for others. Help me move beyond restitution to the healing state of reconciliation.

Reflection: Are there situations in your life where a paper crane, a "forgiveness party," or some other expression of a desire for reconciliation would be appropriate? When in your family history did you experience what the forgiving parent and prodigal child experienced? Is there a situation now that might be improved if members of your family would do the same?

Songs: "My Son Has Gone Away" (Bob Dufford)
Books: *Weasel* by Cynthia DeFelice (New York: Simon & Schuster Childrens), WF; *Strength to Love* by Martin Luther King, Jr. (Minneapolis, MN: Augsburg Fortress, 1981), A
Videos: *The War* (example of alternatives to revenge), WF; *Ulee's Gold* (a modern-day parable of the prodigal son and the forgiving nature of family), T/A

4. Letting Go and Moving On

You shall not take vengeance or bear a grudge. (Leviticus 19:18)

Love…is not resentful. (1 Corinthians 13:5)

Injuries are often hard to forgive and impossible to forget. A too easy forgiveness can often mask the hurt or push the feelings of resentment deeper into the heart. But at some time, we need to let go of these hurts and get on with our lives. Grudges keep us chained; we are not free until we can let them go.

We often hear relatives of murder victims say things like: "I won't have peace or resolution until they execute that killer." We can understand such feelings and can identify with the pain behind the angry words. But it's people like Don who convinced me that there is no real freedom and resolution until someone has the courage and compassion to seek reconciliation instead of revenge. Don spoke humbly of his three-year struggle to begin a process of reconciliation with a young man who had raped and killed his nineteen-year-old daughter. This forgiving witness is transforming the small Midwest town where all the parties live. Don is freeing others as well as himself to challenge the violence in his community with courage and love.

It pains me to watch young people hold on to grudges. I feel sorry for them because they are prisoners of their own worst feelings. I see grown children holding grudges against their parents and siblings, wasting so much energy in negativity. Grudges color our whole personality, leaving us bitter instead of better.

Life is too short and too precious to squander it in resentment. Some families encourage one another to write down hurts that bother them and to put these pieces of paper into a "grudge jar" to help them let go of what could become a long-term grudge.

Again, though, it is good to remember that an easy apology, without some restitution and a firm purpose of amendment, won't do the job. Victims of abuse know that momentary remorse and promises to change are meaningless without clear steps to make amends, to change one's behavior, and to address the issues underlying the abusive behavior.

Prayer: Jesus, you experienced a lot of painful hurts. Your own townspeople wouldn't accept you. In fact, they ran you out of town and tried to kill you. Many who started to follow you walked away when your message didn't suit them. In your crisis, one of your closest disciples betrayed you, another denied even knowing you, and the rest fled. But you knew you were loved by God, and you remained firm in that love. You found the courage and compassion to forgive and to work with your future leaders despite their failings. And you do all this for me as well. Thank God you don't hold a grudge every time I let you down. Help me remember this. Maybe I will let go of any lingering grudges and turn this negative energy into positive energy in your service.

Reflection: Are there hurts you brood over? What could you do to let go of those hurts and move on? If not a "grudge jar," what other symbol or mechanism for letting go of grudges would work for your family or other intimate circles?

Songs: "How Can I Keep from Singing" (traditional); "Lift Every Voice" (traditional); "Love Is" (Elton John)
Books: *A Real Winner* by Patricia and Frederick McKissack (St. Louis: Milliken, 1987; overcoming a "bully"), WF; *Mr. Ives' Christmas* by Oscar Hijuelos (New York: HarperCollins, 1996), T/A; *Dead Man Walking* by Helen Prejean (New York: Vintage Books, 1994), T/A; *Forgive and Forget: Healing the Hurts We Don't Deserve* by Lewis Smedes (New York: Harper and Row, 1996), A
Videos: *Dead Man Walking* (Sister Helen Prejean's ministry of reconciliation), T/A

5. The Courage to Forgive
Don Mosley

"Forgive, and you will be forgiven." (Luke 6:37)

For you, O Lord, are good and forgiving, / abounding in steadfast love to all who call on you. (Psalm 86:5)

For ye were enemies and Allah joined your hearts in love, so that by His Grace ye became brethren. (Qur'an 3:103)

Sabina was sixteen years old when she and her family arrived in the United States. They were refugees, Bosnian Muslims driven from their home by the brutality of war—the "ethnic cleansing" of the Serbs. But seldom would you guess that, seeing Sabina's bright smile and listening to her excited chatter in broken English. She seemed to absorb the new language without effort.

They came to live with us at Jubilee Partners, a Christian service community in northeast Georgia that has hosted refugees from all over the world. More than three hundred of them have been Bosnian Muslims, all with scars in their spirits, hurts too deep to be expressed. For two months Sabina and her family studied English intensively in our classes while their spirits began the long healing process from the violence they had experienced.

Shortly after Sabina arrived, we hosted a group called Murder Victims' Families for Reconciliation. These people have experienced the tragic loss of relatives or close friends who have been murdered. What makes these people special is their discovery that healing involves forgiving the murderer. As they travel around speaking to groups, other people make the same discovery.

George White, an MVFR member, spoke to the Jubilee community one evening. In an emotional presentation, he told us of the night a man shot both him and his wife in a robbery attempt. His wife died instantly, and the gunman escaped without leaving a clue. Somehow the jury decided that George had killed his wife and then wounded himself to appear innocent. He spent years in prison before he managed to prove his innocence. During that time the faithful love of his teenage son and daughter helped him keep his sanity. They also helped him forgive the killer and all those who had misjudged him and almost destroyed his life.

I watched Sabina listen intently to George's story. "Could you understand?" I asked her. "Yes, I understand, but I don't understand. A man kills your wife, and you forgive that man? I don't understand how it is possible!" Her eyes filled with tears. "I hope I can forgive the Serbs like that in ten years."

I called George over and told him what Sabina had said. He put his hands on her shoulders and looked at her through his own tears. "Honey, you have to try. It's the only way to heal from this mess." Then the Christian man from Alabama and the Muslim teenager from Bosnia tearfully hugged, and grew stronger.

Prayer: Dear God, you love even those who commit the worst atrocities. Help us to be enough like you that we learn to forgive those who wrong us, beginning with the trivial offenses and growing as we practice.

Reflection: What can you do if you just don't feel able to forgive someone for something he or she did to you? How can you help family members or friends move toward this kind of forgiveness?

Songs: "Peace Prayer of Saint Francis" (John Foley); "Be Reconciled As One" (Willcock); "Mighty Lord" (John Foley)
Books: *Blood Brothers* by Elias Chacour and David Hazard (Old Tappan, NJ: Chosen Books, 1987; forgiveness in the Middle East), T/A; *Oasis of Peace* by Laurie Dolphin (New York: Scholastic Books, 1993; story-picture book of Arabs and Jews living together), WF; *Beirut Diary* by Sis Levin (Downers Grove, IL: InterVarsity

Press, 1989; the story of Sis' pursuit of her husband kidnapped in Beirut and their pursuit of forgiveness), T/A
Videos: *Murder Close Up* (Mennonite Media Productions, see page 123; several MVFM stories), T/A

6. Apologize and Make Amends

*"I will get up and go to my [parents], and I will say to [them],
'...I have sinned against heaven and before you.'"* (Luke 15:18)

*Kind words and covering of faults are better than charity
followed by injury.* (Qur'an 2:263)

We often take out our frustrations—regardless of their origins—on those closest to us. Spouses do it with each other and/or with their children; children often do the same with younger siblings. In fact, there may be times when "I'm sorry" is the only thing that keeps us in contact with those we love.

Saying "I'm sorry" is one of the most important phrases in any language. Will I "lose face," get taken advantage of, or be rebuffed if I apologize? Maybe, but I will eventually lose a whole lot more if I don't learn how to be humble, to accept my limitations, and to apologize when I wrong another.

There are lots of ways to say "I'm sorry." Speaking the words face to face, with sorrow in our eyes and in our hearts, is the most direct. For many people, however, a written apology delivers a fuller statement than words might permit; writing words often frees people for verbal comment or interpretation later on. Some people are good at giving gifts and knowing what, how, and when to extend a "gift" apology.

But there are times when words and gestures are not enough—especially if there are no efforts to change behavior and/or make amends. There is no real reconciliation without some sort of restitution. Victims of abuse—including family members of an alcoholic or drug-addicted member—certainly have the right to walk away from apologies that are not backed up by a change in behavior.

Yes, Jesus says we are to forgive seventy times seven, but he does not tell us to remain in abusive situations. In fact, Jesus spells out the stages for us to follow if a person's behavior needs correcting. First, we are to confront the person in private. If that doesn't work, we are to provide witnesses or others who can help the person see the error of his or her ways. If that still doesn't work, we are to go to a higher authority, like the Church. Finally, if that doesn't work, we are to treat the person as an outsider, even sever our relationship with that person if need be. While Jesus might not have intended this four-stage process to apply to every relationship, especially permanent relationships like families, it does offer insight for people in hurtful family situations.

Prayer: Jesus, help me to be humble, willing to apologize, make amends, and change any hurtful behavior. Please help me, too, to find the courage and compassion to confront hurtful behavior as you would.

Reflection: Have you caused a hurt for which you need to apologize and/or make amends? How can you instill in your family a greater willingness to apologize and make amends?

Songs: "Amazing Grace" (traditional); "Be Reconciled as One" (Willcock); "There Is a River" (Tim Manion)

Books: *Let's Be Friends Again* by Hans Wilhelm (New York: Scholastic Books, 1988), WF; *Seventy Times Seven* by Johann Arnold (Farmington, PA: Plough Publishing House, 1997), A; also helpful, the Twelve Step Program of Alcoholics Anonymous (World Services Inc., P.O. Box 459, Grand Central Station, NY 10163; 212-870-3400)

Videos: *Broadway Danny Rose* (a woman seeks Danny's forgiveness by repeating his own philosophy of "forgiveness, acceptance, and love"), T/A

7. Atonement for Privileges

"Father, forgive them; for they do not know what they are doing." (Luke 23:34)

For three transgressions of Israel, / and for four, I will not revoke the punishment; / because they sell the righteous for silver. (Amos 2:6)

The stories Nicaraguan mothers told of the killing of their loved ones during the "Contra war" deeply touched well-known spiritual guide Henri Nouwen in 1983. Realizing that these Contra rebels were supplied with money and weapons from the United States, Nouwen asked these mothers for forgiveness for these policies and for his own silent complicity and privileged lifestyle. He encountered the crucified Christ in the sufferings of these women. His atonement (at-one-ment), begun during his two-week visit to Nicaragua, continued through his talks, articles, advocacy efforts, and willingness to deepen his simple lifestyle.

When we allow ourselves to listen to the voices of the poor, we are faced with our relatively privileged lifestyle and the political policies that protect these lifestyles at the expense of others. The Presbyterian Church USA developed a program to help those who are privileged respond to their privilege. Through its "Two Cents a Meal" program, participants put two cents in a box for each meal served at their dinner table. These boxes are then brought to worship monthly, where families have their children carry the boxes to the altar. Proceeds are divided among local food pantries and groups like Church World Services. It isn't the few dollars that make a difference as much as the increased awareness the impact our privileged lifestyle has on others and the need to find ways of making amends for that injustice. The dailiness of these tiny sacrifices also helps change hearts.

We can discover many other tiny privileges to relinquish, like drinking water rather than soft drinks, forgoing snacks from vending machines, and resisting expensive brand-name items. Some families address this issue of economic privilege by implementing an "exchange policy." Whenever a new piece of clothing is purchased, for instance, the individual donates an older piece of clothing to a group that helps those in need. Many families with surplus wealth tithe generously. Others live as simply as possible.

But just as Henri Nouwen realized his apology must lead him to confront government policies, so we, too, must consider participating in consumer boycotts of corporations providing goods and services at the expense of exploited workers or an exploited environment. We can become part of the Families Against Violence Advocacy Network (see page 118), Bread for the World, or the Children's Defense Fund, and follow their political action guidelines for shaping more just public policies.

Like those who participated in Jesus' crucifixion, we often "know not what we do." We don't allow ourselves to see Jesus in those who are hungry or in sorrowful Nicaraguan mothers.

Prayer: Jesus, it's hard to care about people so far away. It's hard to see the connections between our comfort and the discomfort of others. Give us eyes to see, hearts to care, and the courage to make amends for the unjust privileges we enjoy.

Reflection: What privileges do you enjoy—because of your economic class, race, or gender—that come at the expense of others? Can you renounce them in some way or challenge the injustice underlying them? What is one way your whole family might let go of an unjust privilege you enjoy?

Songs: "Look Beyond the Refugee" (*Jubilee*, see page 120); "Satisfied Mind" (Hays/Rhodes); "Go Down, Moses" (African-American spiritual)
Books: *A Country Far Away* by Nigel Gray(New York: Orchard Books, 1989; life of US children counterpoised with children in Third World settings), WF
Videos: *The Power of One* (a white South African youth joins the struggle against Apartheid), T/A; *Salvador* (US journalist transformed by his experience in El Salvador), T/A

CHRIST OF THE AMERICAS

Part V
Respect Nature

To treat the environment and all living things, including our pets, with respect and care

1. "All God's Critters Got a Place in the Choir"

God saw everything that [God] had made, and indeed, it was very good. (Genesis 1:31)

Lack of respect for growing living things soon leads to lack of respect for humans too. (Chief Luther Standing Bear)

We sent thee not, but as a mercy for all creatures. (Qur'an 21:107)

Many church camp families are familiar with the song "All God's Critters Got a Place in the Choir." This playful, musical, religious insight reminds us of the sacredness of all life, from the smallest species of insects to the largest species of mammals and trees. While God has created the human species as special in many ways, God's "choir" isn't complete without the full complement of species. Each species is a unique revelation of the infinite beauty and goodness of God. Human cruelty, meanness, or carelessness toward any plant or animal is a form of violence and sometimes leads to violence toward other humans. What children and adults do to defenseless forms of tiny life they may well attempt to do to physically weaker human beings as well. Conversely, learning to treat plant and animal forms of life with appreciation and reverence inclines us to appreciate and reverence our human sisters and brothers.

As a young adult, I worked as a counselor with troubled teenage boys, many of whom were violent. An integral part of their rehabilitation was being assigned a pet. Each youth was fully responsible for the care of his pet. In return they experienced a loyalty many of them had never known.

There are many other ways to cultivate a sense of appreciation and reverence for creation. "No impact" and "low impact" camping and hiking, for example, keep God's wilderness available for future generations of humans. Parents, grandparents, aunts, and uncles might invite the young people in their lives to help tend a family garden. Creative parents and teachers of young children do things like a "Save the Worms Day" after a heavy spring rain. Children and adults rescue worms from the sidewalks and/or driveways and put them back into their earthy homes. Where appropriate, planting a tree for each child in your life, sharing that tree with the child, and inviting the child to help care for the tree draws the youngster into a deeper relationship with a part of Mother Earth.

Thinking and speaking of creation in personal terms can similarly deepen these relationships. Francis of Assisi sang of Brother Sun and Sister Moon. Native peoples of every continent often refer to creation in similar terms. Familiar words attributed to Chief Seattle implore adults to "teach your children that the rivers are our brothers, and yours....But the white man treats his mother, the earth, and his brother, the sky, as things to be bought, plundered.... His appetite will devour the earth and leave behind only a desert."

Prayer: Creator God, your infinite beauty and goodness are so manifest in the mountains, rivers, and oceans of this world. But they are equally revealed in the species of life that inhabit these magnificent homes. Help us to see, appreciate, and reverence you in every creature, large and small. And help us pass on this way of living to the young people in our lives.

Reflection: How can you nurture in your own soul this sense of reverence for all species of life? How can your family grow together in appreciation for the whole of God's creation?

Songs: "All God's Critters Got a Place in the Choir" (*Rainbow People*, see page 120)

Books: *Brother Eagle, Sister Sky* by Susan Jeffers, illustrator (New York: Dial Press, 1991), WF

Videos: *Gorillas in the Mist* (the story of Dian Fossey's work with gorillas in Africa), WF

2. Gentle Down by Savoring Creation

"Blessed are the meek, for they will inherit the earth." (Matthew 5:5)

Beauty is before me and beauty is behind me. Above and below me hovers the beautiful. I am surrounded by it. I am immersed in it. In my youth I am aware of it. And in old age I shall walk quietly the beautiful trail. (Navajo Prayer from *Earth Prayers,* by Elizabeth Roberts, San Francisco: Harper and Row, 1991)

The enjoyment of earthly beauty is not just the inheritance of or reward for those who are already meek; it is a path by which we can become meek. The familiar phrase "Music soothes the savage beast" can be equally applied to nature; beauty, too, soothes the savage beast in us.

We all have the potential for violent eruption. After a frustrating day at work or school, for example, with traffic jammed, and weather or accidents altering our plans—one of those terrible, horrible, no-good, very bad days—we feel our threshold for an angry outburst not far away. At times like that, we need to gentle down. We need a place and moment of beauty, enhanced perhaps with gentle music. This daily "sabbatical," perhaps only ten or fifteen minutes, does for our spirits what the Sabbath does for our week.

The curative, gentling power of nature is so evident in the beauty of a flower, a garden, a special plant, or a simple tree. Sitting in silence with this beauty releases the tension built up over a hectic or frustrating day. Such silent sitting also helps orient our day at sunrise. Nature's power for gentling us down is an effective antidote to the violence we find in ourselves.

I recommend the following places for such beauty. First, I recommend a place in your home or apartment—perhaps just a special flower or a picture of beauty—where you can absorb some beauty every day of the year. I suggest this for your work place as well. Second, I recommend a space outdoors where you can enjoy some natural beauty whenever the season and weather permits. Third, I recommend that you seek out special places in your community—like parks, gardens, trails—where you can enjoy a weekly sabbatical to gentle down. Finally, I recommend special places of beauty when traveling—places that generate and nurture a peaceful spirit.

Jesus lives most of his active ministry outdoors; he prays in gardens and on mountaintops, and preaches on hillsides and lakeshores. His manner and message are enhanced by his surroundings, and his listeners are offered wholeness in the wholesomeness of the hillsides. The gentle spirit and power of Francis and Clare of Assisi were similarly nurtured outdoors in communion with God's creation.

Prayer: Jesus, Francis, and Clare, lure us into the beauty of creation where we can be gentled and healed. Help us add some senseless acts of beauty to some random acts of kindness we commit each day. And help us take some of the many opportunities we have to lead our children, grandchildren, nieces, and nephews into this world of beauty and gentleness.

Reflection: What opportunities does natural beauty offer you for a daily, weekly, and yearly gentling down and healing? How can you make natural beauty more a part of the lives of all the people to whom you are close?

Songs: "Simple Gifts" (*Rainbow People*, see page 120); "Peace Is Flowing Like a River" (Carey Landry); "Rocky Mountain High" (John Denver)
Books: *The Sense of Wonder* by Rachel Carson (New York: Harper and Row, 1965), T/A; *One Light, One Sun* by Raffi (New York: Crown, 1988), WF
Videos: *Brother Sun, Sister Moon* (the life of Francis of Assisi), WF

Violence Ends Where **LOVE** Begin

3. Nature Is Where You Find Your God

The heavens are telling the glory of God; / and the firmament proclaims [God's] handiwork. (Psalm 19:1)

My profession is to be always on the alert to find God in nature, to know God's lurking places. (John Muir)

Early in his life, John Muir discovered God in creation. Over the years, he was led deeper, place by place, moment by moment, into this sacred presence. As a result, his life has inspired millions, leading them to discover for themselves God's sacred presence and hear God's voice with a clarity to match the clarity of the landscape. Native Americans have always understood this truth and have sent their youth on vision quests as part of their maturation, to listen to the Great Spirit and discover their strengths and sense of direction in life.

What a gift this is for the children in our lives—to lead them to and help them discover God's sacred presence in creation. Some parents have helped their children identify a special place that is theirs to visit whenever they want to listen to God. This place is used to mark significant moments in the faith development and maturation of the child.

For our children, this was on the occasions of their first Communion and confirmation. At those times, we went with them into nature to reflect on the significance of that particular sacramental moment in their lives. One Lutheran family steeped in Native American traditions used the practice of a vision quest for their son's confirmation at age sixteen. His mother drove him to the site he had chosen for this twenty-four-hour experience. The youngster pitched his tent and Mom gave her son his water supply for his twenty-four-hour fast. The next evening his family and other families in their small faith community joined the youngster for a ceremony and feast. Around a fire, the young man shared what he had been given during the experience. Then each adult blessed him and welcomed him into the community of adult believers.

Whether we are children or adults, we will respect and appreciate nature if we regularly experience God's sacred presence there; we will, very naturally, celebrate God's presence and live more joyfully and prayerfully. We will probably try to simplify our lives to live more in harmony with the earth and be more careful about our use of its resources. And we are much more likely to stand in defense of creation. Words attributed to Chief Seattle remind us of our generational responsibility: "Teach your children what we have taught our children, that the earth is our mother. Whatever befalls the earth, befalls the sons and daughters of the earth."

Prayer: O beautiful Creator God, we stand in awe before the splendor of your creation. We sense your sacred presence and pause to listen to your voice. Attune all our senses to your presence. Help us gentle down so that we can truly discover and savor your sacred presence. Help us to see the importance of sharing this experience with the next generation and to make the time to do so.

Reflection: Where do you go, or could you go, to experience and savor God's sacred presence in nature? How can you make this experience a family or group event?

Songs: "Canticle of the Sun" (Marty Haugen); "All the Ends of the Earth" (Bob Dufford); "Let Us Break Bread Together" (African-American spiritual); "Jesus in the Morning" (African-American spiritual)
Books: *Earth Prayers* by Elizabeth Roberts (San Francisco: Harper and Row, 1991), A; *Listening to Nature: How to Deepen your Awareness of Nature* by Joseph Cornell (Nevada City, CA: Dawn Publications, 1987), WF
Videos: *Grand Canyon* (a taste of its beauty), T/A

4. Nurture Nonviolence through Nature

All of this [the earth] is sacred and so do not forget! Every dawn as it comes is a holy event, and every day is holy. (from a Oglala Sioux ritual)

"...that they may all be one." (John 17:21)

G andhi once described nonviolence as "the power that manifests itself in us when we become aware of the oneness of life." Through his many "experiments with truth" (also the title of his autobiography), Gandhi deepened and broadened his loving heart to such a degree that he radiated love even to his opponents. They knew he cared for them at the same time he resisted their policies and practices. It is not surprising to learn that Gandhi spent time each day in prayerful union with creation and the Creator.

Not only does nature have the power to gentle us down, it draws us into communion with all life. Communion with the whole of creation leads to communion with the human species. There are special places and times for such communion. Perhaps the two most popular and available times are sunrise and sunset. Some describe these as God's two great performances every day, and they make sure that God does not "play to an empty house." Perhaps you've seen it: the dark predawn sky that gradually takes on colors—pinks, reds, yellows. You sense the sun inching its way up the horizon until it explodes in an ecstacy of light. We can savor this moment as Francis did, singing out to Brother Sun and feeling the warmth of God's love in the radiance of the sun.

Then again at sunset, after the cares and challenges of the day have been embraced, we are again carried into this spectacle of light as colors climb upward and the sun sinks into the horizon. Our hearts expand in this moment of swelling color. Our hearts want to break into song—"Then sings my soul, my Savior God to thee, how great thou art, how great thou art."

In that moment we touch a unity with all creation: "We are one in the Spirit, we are one in the Lord…and we pray that all unity may one day be restored." That unity is being restored in us, in that very moment. Jesus' prayer "that they may all be one" is being realized in our very selves in that moment. God's great plan for the world—"the reunification of all things in Christ" (see Ephesians 1:10)—is being realized in that moment of communion.

Prayer: Awesome Creator God, how great thou art! Lead us to you through every moment and movement of life. Help us to savor your creation as the revelation and celebration of your love. Make us, your humble creatures, also revelations and celebrations of your love. Make us, as you made your servants Gandhi and Francis, a means of your peace.

Reflection: What places and moments of communion can you make a part of your daily routine? How can you nurture this sense of quiet communion within your family or other small groups?

Songs: "How Great Thou Art" (Stuart K. Hine); "Awesome God" (Rich Mullin); "Sunshine" (John Denver); "May There Always Be Sunshine" (*Rainbow People*, see page 120); "Listen" (*Teaching Peace*, see page 120)
Books: *The Way to Start a Day* by Byrd Baylor (Emeryville, CA: Children's Book Press, 1978), WF; *The Universe Is a Green Dragon* by Brian Swimme (Santa Fe, NM: Bear & Co., 1984), A;

Journey and the Dream by Murray Bodo (Cincinnati: St. Anthony Messenger Press, 1972; meditations on Francis of Assisi), T/A
Videos: *Brother Sun, Sister Moon* (the life of Francis of Assisi), WF

5. Give Back to Nature in Gratitude

The Lord God [put the human] in the garden of Eden to till it and keep it. (Genesis 2:15)

Whoever plants a tree and diligently looks after it until it matures and bears fruit is rewarded. The world is green and bountiful and God has appointed you as stewards over it. (Muhammed)

The earth does not belong to us; we belong to the earth. (Chief Seattle)

The Legend of the Bluebonnet by Tomie DePaulo is a children's story with a grown-up message. The Comanche people in Texas suffer through a severe draught that claims the lives of the parents of a young Comanche girl named "She Who Is Alone." In desperation, the people send the holy man to the mountaintop to pray to the Great Spirit to send the rains. The holy man returns and tells the people that they have been selfish; they have taken from the earth without giving back. He tells them that someone must sacrifice his or her best thing as an act of reparation. When all the adult Comanches find excuses, She Who Is Alone decides that maybe her best (and only) thing, the warrior doll with a blue feather that she received from her uncle, could be offered in reparation. That night the young girl goes to the mountain, builds a fire, and places her doll in it; the ashes she sprinkles in the four sacred directions. When she awakens at dawn, the hillsides are covered with bluebonnets (from the blue feather) and by midday the rains come. That evening the holy man gathers the people and honors She Who Is Alone with a new name: She Who Dearly Loves Her People.

All of us have been selfish, have taken from the earth, have taken our earth for granted. Many live wastefully, with little regard for future generations. But God has raised up many prophets for the earth in our own time to warn us of the impending destruction and to point the way to an earth-friendly lifestyle. Among these prophets are Chief Seattle, John Muir, Rachel Carson, and the Lorax—a fictional Dr. Seuss character who speaks for the trees as powerfully and effectively to children as John Muir has to adults. Then there is Johnny Appleseed and Muhammed. All these voices say the same thing—plant trees!

There are many tree planting projects and groups for schools and communities. Adults are planting trees to honor the children in their lives. Adults and children alike are joining groups working to protect the forests in their state, province, or country.

Each tree is a spire of praise, stretching forth its arms toward its Creator. The giant sequoias are the largest living beings on earth and are up to 2700 years old. What awesome revelations of the grandeur of their Creator! What an awesome privilege and responsibility it is to speak for such trees.

Prayer: Awesome Creator God, you give us such a glorious creation to enjoy, to enhance, and to pass on to future generations. Help us to find the wisdom, generosity, and courage to be prophetic stewards standing in defense of your creation.

Reflection: How have you been selfish toward the earth and what could you do to turn this around? How can your family, faith community, and other groups you are in give back to the earth?

Songs: "Inch by Inch" (*Rainbow People*, see page 120); "On This Day the First of Days" (Lubeck)

Books: *The Legend of the Bluebonnet* by Tomie DePaulo (New York: Scholastic Books, 1983), WF; *Son of the Wilderness: The Life of John Muir* by Linnie Marsh Wolfe (Madison, WI: University of Wisconsin Press, 1978), T/A; *Johnny Appleseed* by Steven Kellogg (New York: Morrow, 1988), WF

Videos: *Mosquito Coast* (a look at the Amazon rain forest), T/A; *Amazing Grace and Chuck* (sacrificing to save the earth), WF

6. A Debt to the Future

Ken Lovingood

Like good stewards of the manifold grace of God, serve one another with whatever gift each of you has received. (1 Peter 4:10)

Teach your children what we have taught our children, that the earth is our mother...Care for it as we have cared for it...And with all your strength, with all your mind, with all your heart, preserve it for your children, and love it as God loves us all. (Chief Seattle)

The earth, a wonderful place, is our only place to live right now and into the future. But it is a fragile place, vulnerable to our excesses. Most of us either race along using the earth's resources at an alarming rate or we are pulled along by the rest. Only recently have we begun to realize that this vessel has limited resources. God did not make it as infinite as God is.

Native Americans, of which my ancestors were part, knew this. Either they were close to the earth and the rest of nature, or God chose to speak to them more directly than to us in this age. It is for good reason that we all should listen to the earth and learn to treat it as if it were on loan to us, to be passed to future generations.

Close your eyes and take a deep breath. Breathe in the air that clings to this earth and gives you life. Give thanks to God, however you envision God. Touch a stone or a piece of wood; feel the substance of it. Give thanks to God for its reality and the gift it is to you. Dip your hand in water, cool or warm, and give thanks to God for its soothing, healing, encompassing presence. Thank God for this gift that renews itself in every rainstorm and dewdrop.

Our Native American ancestors also knew, and remind us, that all these things—and many more—are ours to have as stewards, not lords. They are only on loan to us for a while. God wants us to pass them on to those who are just waiting to walk this earth with us or after we have passed to another place.

In the epilogue of *Wisdom Keepers*, by Steve Wall and Harvey

Arden, Leon Shenandoah talks about the seventh generation. "The future we learned was not some abstract untouchable 'beyond' far out there somewhere beyond our ken. Rather, the Wisdom Keepers taught us, the future is here today in the now and here. It is coming up, in fact, behind you. 'Look over your shoulder, Tadodaho,' Leon Shenendoah told us. 'Look behind you. See your sons and daughters; these are your future. Look further and see your sons' and daughters' children and their children's children even unto the seventh generations. Think about it! You yourself are a seventh generation!'"

Prayer: Dear Great Spirit God, one God with many names, show me the way to care for the earth and all its wonders. Help me to pay the debt that I have incurred because I have enjoyed the fruits of the earth. Help me preserve it for all who are here and all yet to come.

Reflection: "Be a steward of the earth. Preserve it for your children." What does this mean to you? How can your family or community practice better stewardship as a part of your daily routine? If you thought about the impact of your lifestyle over the next seven generations, what changes would you make?

Songs: "Sing to the Mountains" (Bob Dufford)
Books: *Wisdom Keepers* by Steve Wall and Harvey Arden, (Hillsboro, OR: Beyond Words Publishing Co., 1990), A; *Why the Sky Is Far Away: A Nigerian Folktale* by Mary Joan Gerson (Little, Brown and Co., 1992), WF; *This Year's Garden* by Cynthia Rylant (New York: Bradbury, 1984; a family's caring for the earth), WF
Videos: *Dances with Wolves* (the beauty and simplicity of Native American life close to the earth), T/A

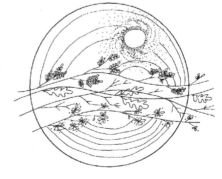

7. Eat with Gratitude and Relish

So, whether you eat or drink, or whatever you do, do everything for the glory of God. (1 Corinthians 10:31)

In this food, I see clearly the presence of the entire universe supporting my existence. (Thich Nhat Hanh, from *Present Moment, Wonderful Moment*)

In the old days the hunter sang to the deer that he knew the deer's life was as precious as his, but he must kill, so his children could have food to eat. He explained that the deer's life would continue in his body. (Navajo elder, quoted in *Song of the Earth Spirit* by Susanne Anderson, New York: McGraw Hill, 1973)

G andhi was the model of nonviolence in the twentieth century, but this was not an easy inheritance. He had to work at overcoming his own propensity to self-gratification and violence. As he said, "I have not the shadow of a doubt that any man or woman can achieve what I have, if he or she would make the same effort and cultivate the same hope and faith."

Gandhi strove daily to live a life of integrity. He experimented in every facet of living, including eating. Learning how to eat with integrity, with gratitude, and in harmony with all of life led him into several areas of nonviolence. First, convinced that nonviolence required a mastery over his bodily desires and a deep dedication to service, Gandhi often fasted to purify and focus himself on the needs of others. Second, he experimented with vegetarianism. His sense of reverence for life prohibited the killing of animals for his own consumption.

Many practitioners of nonviolence have followed Gandhi's example, seeking a diet that nourishes their bodies and spirits at the least expense to the rest of creation. One of the beauties of a fruit-and-vegetable diet, for example, is that it can be provided locally, sometimes collectively, often in our own backyards, and with little expense to the rest of creation. Hunters from many indigenous traditions reflect this respect in their prayer to the spirits of the animals they have to kill to feed their families, promising to ingest their spirits and eat them in humble gratitude.

No matter where we get our food, we can prepare it carefully and savor it gratefully. "Eating on the run," as we sometimes do, deprives us of this opportunity for harmony with the earth.

Prayer: Jesus, you feasted and fasted, and you made yourself available to us in a "eucharistic banquet." When it's time for a feast, help us share it with others and enjoy it with gratitude. But when we sense that we are living too much for ourselves, help us to fast and refocus our lives on service to others. Help us be more careful about what we eat—its effects on our health and on the whole of creation. Help us to enjoy every meal we have, relishing it and the fellowship that meal time can provide.

Reflection: How could you eat with more integrity and gratitude and in harmony with the rest of creation? How can meal time in your family or community become a more joyful experience?

Songs: "Simple Gifts" (*Rainbow People,* see page 120); "Hurray for the World" (*Teaching Peace,* see page 120); "Slow Down, You're Movin' Too Fast" (Paul Simon); "Hope in a Hopeless World" (Widespread Panic)

Books: *The Miracle of the Potato Latkes* by Malka Penn (New York: Holiday House, 1994; poor Jewish woman shares what food she has), WF; *Diet for a New America* and *May All Be Fed* by John Robbins (Santa Cruz, CA: EarthSave, 1989 and 1992), A; *The Man Who Killed the Deer* by Frank Waters (Athens, OH: Swallow Press, 1995), T/A

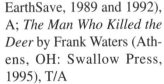

Videos: *Gandhi* (a profile of his simple and grateful lifestyle as part of his nonviolent struggle for true freedom), T/A

8. Stand in Defense of Creation

The earth is the Lord's and all that is in it. (Psalm 24:1)

The whole creation has been groaning. (Romans 8:22)

Sierra Blanca is a small town in Texas, near the Rio Grande River. Forty percent of its residents live below the poverty level and two-thirds are Mexican-American. Sierra Blanca is also the proposed site for a dumping ground for nuclear power plants. Under a compact that Texas entered into with the states of Maine and Vermont, radioactive wastes from aging nuclear power plants could be transported across the nation to Sierra Blanca.

Because of serious environmental and health dangers, residents of the area organized, and Congress defeated the first Texas-Maine-Vermont compact proposed in 1995. Plans like these keep coming back, however, especially in economically poor communities heavily populated with people of color. Environmental racism extends overseas as well, as wealthy countries and corporations dump their dangerous products into vulnerable societies.

As Scripture says, the whole of creation is groaning. Hearing these groans and the biblical mandate to be stewards of God's creation, people are taking collective action in defense of creation. This sense of corporate stewardship is captured in the Preamble of the "Earth Covenant: A Citizens' Treaty for Common Ecological Security," offered to the world by Global Education Associates in the early 1990s: "We, the peoples of the Earth, rejoice in…life in all its diversity. Earth is our home. We share it with all other living beings. Yet we are rendering the Earth uninhabitable.… Lands are becoming barren, skies fouled, waters poisoned. The cry of people whose land, livelihood, and health are being destroyed is heard around the world. The Earth itself is calling us to awaken. We and all living beings depend upon the Earth and upon one another.…Our common future depends upon a reexamination of our most basic assumptions about humankind's relationship to the Earth. We must develop common principles and systems to shape this future in harmony with the Earth. Governments alone cannot secure the environment. As citizens of the world, we accept responsibility in our personal, occupational and community lives, to protect the integrity of the Earth."

The "Earth Covenant" concludes with a call to "work for the enactment of laws that protect the environment and promote their observance through educational, political, and legal action." All of us can increase our corporate effectiveness by joining local or national organizations like the National Wildlife Federation, the Sierra Club, or others described in *The Green Consumer* action guide.

Part of our collective effort includes passing on this concern to the next generations. Parallel to the "Earth Covenant" is a children's "World Pledge," which might be posted prominently in your home: "I pledge allegiance to the world, to cherish every living thing, to care for earth and sea and air, with peace and freedom everywhere."

Prayer: Creator God, help us to hear the groans of your creation. In the words of the song "In Defense of Creation," *O God, give us courage to stand in defense of creation...give us your breath as we speak in defense of creation...and grant us grace to increase your Shalom as we live in defense of creation.*

Reflection: How can you link more effectively with educational, political, and/or legal efforts in your area in defense of creation? How can you share this concern with children?

Songs: "In Defense of Creation" (*Jubilee*, see page 120); "Hurray for the World" (*Teaching Peace*, see page 120)
Books: *The Lorax* by Dr. Seuss (New York: Random House, 1971), WF; *The Green Consumer* by John Elkington et. Al. (New York:

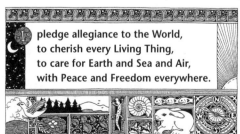

Penguin Books, 1990), A
Videos: *The Lorax* (Dr. Seuss' fictional character speaks for the trees in the face of "progress" fueled by greed), WF

Part VI
Play Creatively

To select entertainment and toys that support our family's values and to avoid entertainment that makes violence look exciting, funny, or acceptable

1. Playful Praise and Praiseful Play

"Whoever does not receive the kingdom of God as a little child will never enter it." (Luke 18:17)

I will sing and make melody... / I will sing praises to you among the nations. (Psalm 108:1,3)

One day, a friend of mine took me to the retreat center where she went during some long months of a difficult divorce. As she showed me around, I found it curious that instead of showing me the indoor chapel where she *prayed*, she showed me the tiny plot of open land where she *played*. Actually, she danced there in that little stretch of land overlooking Puget Sound. She told me how each time she visited the center, she would pour her heart and soul into her ballet as she played before her God. *How God must delight in such playful praise*, I thought.

I went back to that retreat center by myself the next day and, on my own, discovered the basketball court. *Well*, I thought, *if you can praise God dancing, why can't you praise God playing basketball?* When I couldn't find a basketball, the little child in me said, "Ah, go ahead. Play before the Lord, pretending you have a basketball." Well, as you can imagine, I hit three-point shots and graceful hook shots from every spot on the court. At the end of this fifteen-minute prayerful, playful workout, I gave God a "standing o" (ovation). Arms arched over my head, I looked into heaven and into my heart and with a big smile on my face I whispered, "How awesome you are, O lavish, gracious God!" I couldn't help but think that God gave me a "standing o" in return.

On how many mountaintops and at how many sunrise services, wherever God's playful Spirit inspires us to be, do the people of God break forth in this song:

> Morning has broken, like the first morning;
> blackbirds have spoken, like the first bird.

Praise for the singing; praise for the morning;
praise for them springing fresh from your Word.

Yes, playful praise and praiseful play can spring fresh from us each day when we allow the little child in us to uninhibitedly burst forth. No wonder Jesus tells his followers to become like little children. Otherwise they couldn't enter God's realm where God's beloved community delights in playful praise for all eternity.

Most of us first learn to play at home. Then, much later, we get a second chance at play as the children in our lives "keep us young." Unfortunately, as the children get older, family living becomes serious. The issues seem tougher, the kids seem more difficult, parents seem tired, and play slips away. Gone are those grateful, glorious moments of joy that were so prevalent just a few years earlier. Some families, however, don't forget how to play—and not surprisingly, those often are the families that don't forget how to pray.

Prayer: Jesus, help us to play with the enthusiasm of a little child. Help us remember that your God and our God is a God who delights in those sons and daughters who never retire their playful, praiseful spirits.

Reflection: How could you become a more playful, praiseful person? What could you do as a whole family or community to become a more playful, praiseful group?

Songs: "Morning Has Broken" (Cat Stevens); "Play Before the Lord" (Bob Dufford)

Books: *Sharing Nature with Children* by Joseph Cornell (Nevada City, CA: Dawn Publications, 1979), T/A
Videos: *Shall We Dance?* (a Japanese businessman learns the joy of dance), T/A

2. "O How We Could Harmonize"

For the Lord *your God is bringing you into a good land, a land with flowing streams, with springs and underground waters welling up in valleys and hills...a land of olive trees and honey...a land where you lack nothing.* (Deuteronomy 8:7,8,9)

And the Lord *God planted a garden in Eden...and there [God] put the [human] whom [God] had formed.* (Genesis 2:8)

According to the Book of Genesis, God created us to play in a garden, in harmony with the rest of creation. But God gave freedom to the humans and, sure enough, we wanted more than to live in creaturely harmony.

Yet humans have used that same freedom to remember God's garden dream. We are learning how to harmonize and live in unison. This is especially true when we take our play outdoors and hike our way into the heart of this garden earth. Hiking is much more than getting to the top of something or the end of something as fast as we can. As Robert Pirsig put it, "You climb the mountain with an equilibrium between restlessness and exhaustion. Then, when you are no longer thinking ahead, each footstep isn't just a means to an end but a unique event in itself" (from *The Earth Speaks* by Steve Van Matre, Greenville, WV, Institute for Earth Education, 1983).

Vietnamese Buddhist monk Thich Nhat Hanh, in a meditation on the art of walking, encourages us to harmonize our breathing with the steps we take. He also suggests that we try to massage the earth with our feet with each step we take. This kind of harmonious caress is also available whenever we swim in a mountain lake or gentle ocean. Doing a gentle breaststroke, for instance, in rhythm with the water can unite us with that womb-like body of water.

Hiking certainly has helped many, myself included, understand the power and wisdom of the wilderness to reveal God's will, but there are many ways to share this special thrill of communion with our God. We can lead others into similar experiences of the wilderness, or we can take pictures of wilderness beauty and peace around us and share it with others. We can take our photographs a step further, even, and make an "I love the earth" book with them, adding personal reflections and prayers. Wilderness beauty and peace—a revelation of God's gentle love and awesome splendor. What an antidote to violence! What a call to communion!

Prayer: Awesome God, what can we say in the face of such splendor. We fall on our knees in gratitude and commit ourselves to leading others to this experience of your peaceable kingdom, the harmony of your garden where we can flourish as sisters and brothers with the whole of creation.

Reflection: Where do you go—or could you go—to experience the harmony of God's garden? As a family or a community, how can you make such "creation experiences" a major part of your play time together?

Songs: "Happy Wanderer" (*Rainbow People*, see page 120); "Sing a New Song" (Dan Schutte); "Lord of Glory" (Tim Manion); "Woodstock" (Joni Mitchell)
Books: *A Guide to Walking Meditation* by Thich Nhat Hanh, (Nyack, NY: Fellowship of Reconciliation, 1985), T/A; *The Earth Speaks,* Steve Van Matre and Bill Weiler, editor (Greenville, WV: Institute for Earth Education, 1983; an anthology of earth reflec-

tions), T/A; *Fireflies, Fireflies, Light My Way* by Jonathan London (New York: Viking, 1996; images of outdoor beauty), WF
Videos: *The Color Purple* (Shug and her God celebrate purple flowers), T/A

3. The Family that Plays Together Stays Together

"For where two or three are gathered in my name, I am there among them." (Matthew 18:20)

I still proclaim your wondrous deeds. (Psalm 71:17)

One of the saddest commentaries on our time is the proliferation of television sets in bedrooms. So much of our play has become passive and private, as family members scatter to park themselves in front of their own "private" TV sets (or other electronic toys) for their evening and weekend entertainment.

As a boy, I remember kneeling down for our nightly prayers and hearing my parents tell me that "the family that prays together stays together." As an adult with grown children, I have never disagreed with that statement. But I have seen, again and again, that it's also "the family that *plays* together stays together."

When our kids were small, it was easy to get them to play a card game, to go to the zoo or a movie, or to engage in outdoor activities. Now that our children are in their twenties, we find that, once again, we can enjoy those outdoors times from their childhood.

But during their teen years, playing together was very difficult. It was so hard to find the time and, besides, the teens generally preferred to be with their friends. Yet, I do recall a card game that our sons enjoyed even as teens. During some very difficult times with one of our sons, thirty minutes of that card game—the two of us—provided several pleasant memories each week and enabled us to hang in with each other. Playing cards together softened many a confrontation and helped us keep things from getting really ugly.

What a joy it is to discover, as an adult, a game or other activity that you and young people enjoy doing together. One of the most important forms of family play, for example, is storytelling: Bible stories, Dr. Seuss stories, stories of peacemakers and racial justice heroes, family history stories, ghost stories, and other stories that your parents or grandparents made up and shared with you in your youth. My dad had some wonderful characters for his fantasy stories, among them the "Skilary Skalary Alligator" and the "Skeeziks." Oh how I wish I could have remembered them when our kids were young. One promise I hope I keep if I am fortunate enough to enjoy grandparenthood: I want to invent my own episodes for the "Skeeziks" and his friends. (Like some other grandparents, I hope to audiotape and/or videotape these stories so they can be enjoyed by my grandchildren even after their grandfather is gone.)

Prayer: Three-person God, you created us in your image as social beings. You delight in us whenever we remember that you want us to play as much as we pray and work. Keep us together in our play time whenever possible. Help us to delight in one another as much as you delight in us. Help us to remember that when two or three or more of us gather together to play, Jesus is truly in our midst.

Reflection: How can you make your family, work place, or neighborhood more playful? What are the important playful traditions in your family? How could you make them more fun and/or more frequent? What would happen to TV watching as a result?

Songs: "Nobody Ever Gets Killed at Our House" (Charlie King); "Blow Up the TV" (John Prine); "There Is Love" (Paul Stookey)
Books: *Education of Little Tree* by Forrest Carter (Albuquerque,

NM: University of New Mexico Press, 1986), WF; *Self-Help for Kids* (a wonderful catalog of books and games for all ages, Free Spirit Publishing, 1-800-735-7323)
Videos: *Unhook the Stars* (a mother rekindles her zest for life by caring for a troubled youth), T/A

4. Restful Sabbath Play

So God blessed the seventh day and hallowed it, because on it
God rested from all the work that [God] had done in creation.
(Genesis 2:3)

T he Genesis account of creation sets a divine pattern of work
and play, which God apparently intends for us. One day a
week is to be set aside for worship, rest, savoring creation, and
leisurely play.

In its respectful attention to this divine pattern of work and
play, the Jewish celebration of the Sabbath has much to offer all
people of faith. It's the day to refrain from using all those me-
chanical devices that keep us from living as close to nature (natural) as possible. It used to be that stores were closed on Sundays
so people wouldn't have to work and couldn't shoot their Sunday
in shopping. But as mammon and materialism have become idols
for affluent societies, God's weekly pattern has been subverted.

I can understand this subversion, for I was a victim of it for
decades. I loved to worship from 8:00 to 9:00 Sunday morning so
I could have the rest of the day for watching sports, doing chores,
and writing work-related letters. I recall how, at times, a family
celebration felt like an interruption. In those years I had short-
changed my God, my family, myself.

The "Rock" Church changed all this for me. In our late forties,
we discovered this wonderful African-American faith community
whose main worship service is 11:00 a.m. to 1:30 p.m. preceded
and followed by lots of fellowship. Gradually, I learned that this
alteration in my Sabbath day was exactly what God intended.
Rather than a get-it-over-with-as-fast-as-possible one-hour duty,
worship became the center of my day. Then, adding an occasional
brunch with one or two of our grown children or a friend restored
the Sabbath a little further. Having a garden and committing some
Sunday time to its maintenance and enjoyment brought me another step closer to respecting the Sabbath. Leisurely hobbies and
some outdoor fun, if only a pleasant walk, can further enrich the
Sabbath the way I think God intended.

Behind this conversion of activities, of course, is a conversion of attitude. God doesn't judge us, nor should we judge ourselves, on the basis of how much we accomplish but on how much love we put into whatever we accomplish. People, not projects, are the most important. Sabbath worship, play, rest, and family celebrations are part of that balanced good life that God intends for all humans. Distort the Sabbath and we do violence to ourselves. Without the healing elements of the Sabbath, we begin doing violence to others. When we restore the Sabbath, we reduce the violence, not just to humans but to the earth itself.

Prayer: Gracious, lavish God, you wisely showed us how to order our lives. Yet, in our arrogance and desire to do and consume as much as we can, we have violated your way; we have violated ourselves, others, and the rest of your creation. Please help us keep holy your Sabbath day.

Reflection: How might you make your Sabbath day more like the Sabbath God had in mind? What can you do as a whole family or community to enrich your observance of the Sabbath?

Songs: "All I Really Need" (*Rainbow People*, see page 120); "Sing to the Mountains" (Bob Dufford); "This Is the Day" (Michael Joncas); "Sabbath Prayer" (from *Fiddler on the Roof*); "Sing Out, Earth and Sky" (Marty Haugen)

Books: *The Little Prince* by Antoine de Saint-Exupery (New York: Harcourt, Brace and World, 1943), WF

Videos: *Chariots of Fire* (a great runner refuses to race on Sunday), T/A

5. Play as Laughter and Silliness

A cheerful heart is a good medicine, / but a downcast spirit dries up the bones. (Proverbs 17:22)

Then our mouth was filled with laughter, / and our tongue with shouts of joy. (Psalm 126:2)

W here there is laughter, there is little violence. Laughter is an effective antidote to violence and many of its sources: frustration, hurt, depression. Laughter stops an argument midstream. Like a pin to a balloon, it dissipates pent-up anger. We may not know the physiology of laughter, but we do know its results.

Silliness is similar. Children love to act silly. It's sometimes frustrating for adults, but it is also delightful. Silly children are generally not violent children. And children love to see adults being silly. Rolling on the floor together, making silly faces, using silly phrases, or playing silly games—it all lightens up the atmosphere.

So much of life is serious—even our play time—and it's not just the parents of potential Olympic athletes who push their children to become the best. There's nothing wrong with being the best you can be. But there is a difference between "being *your* best" and "being *the* best."

In our highly competitive society, excessive competition often leads to violence. Some coaches and athletes, for example, want blood as well as victory. To them, being #2 means being a loser. Sports should be fun, with winning secondary.

Adults can help bring about this change in perspective in a number of ways. They can carefully order the questions they put to their children after an athletic event the children participated in. First, "Was it fun?" Next, "Did you do your best?" Finally, "What were the results?" They can also encourage cooperative games as a part of family or group playing. Making animal sculptures, for example, or machines out of the bodies of participants are always big hits at family camps. Making fun games a part of extended family celebrations can enrich those celebrations, cut family tensions, put people at ease, and make these events real celebrations.

A family fun night once or twice a month is another way to reduce the possibility of abuse and other forms of destructive behavior within the family. Again, it's hard to laugh and be violent at the same time. The more we laugh, the less we hurt. What a sad commentary on our society to see play reduced to either entertainment or competition, both of which are becoming more violent by the year.

Prayer: Jesus, you delighted in the simplest of things, like flowers and children. You didn't have all the things we do to distract your focus from what is truly important. You probably lightened up every family event you attended. Help us to learn from your Hebrew sages the critical message that a cheerful heart is truly good medicine and that laughter and joyful shouts are really forms of praise, ways we delight our heavenly Parent. Help us reorder our priorities, restore laughter and play to our families, and become like the little children you and our heavenly Parent so delight in.

Reflection: What can you do to insert more laughter and silliness into your life? How does your family or community play together? Are there ways to add more laughter and silliness to this play?

Songs: "Barnyard Boogie" (*Teaching Peace*, see page 120); "Silly Silly Song" and "The Happy Wanderer" (*Rainbow People*, see page 120); "Shake My Sillies Out" (Raffi); "Joy to the World" (Hoyt Axton); "The Lord Has Done Great Things" (Jaime Cortez)

Books: *Just Family Nights,* Susan Vogt, editor (Elgin, IL: Brethren Press, 1994), WF; *Mrs. Gigglebelly Is Coming for Tea* by Donna Guthrie (New York: Simon and Schuster; 1990; a mother's silliness delights her daughter), WF

Videos: *Hook* (a grown-up Peter Pan rediscovers the child within), WF

6. Put Away the Sword (and Swordplay)

Then Jesus said to [Peter], "Put your sword back into its place; for all who take the sword will perish by the sword." (Matthew 26:52)

There's not much in the Bible about violent play. We do know that the early Christians were fed to lions by the Romans for the amusement of crowds in a circus-like setting. But gruesome enjoyment continues unabated today. While we consider ourselves more civilized than the Roman "barbarians," the violence in some of our own forms of entertainment approaches "barbaric" levels.

Along with the escalating levels of violent play, however, are the escalating voices of opposition. Some individuals and families are renouncing violent play altogether: no guns, no war toys, no violent TV shows or videos, no violent sports. Their homes are sometimes marked with a sticker proclaiming it a "violence-free zone." Other families limit violent viewing, play, and toys, without outright bans. Many parents encourage critical viewing skills in their children as they watch TV shows or videos together, raising questions about resolving the conflicts without violence. Some police departments, school districts, faith communities, and other community groups have initiated "buy back" programs for real weapons or toy exchanges for play weapons. The Imani Center in St. Louis, for example, combined this toy gun exchange with a program on the Family Pledge of Nonviolence. At the end of the event, adults and children took the pledge together.

In the face of so much violence, perhaps the time has come for all people of faith to begin a fast from violence and a fast for life, and to declare their home or school or faith community a violence-free zone. It might not seem like a lot, but change doesn't happen overnight. Each step in the right direction is a pebble sending forth ripples whose impact we may never know. We don't control the results; we simply remain faithful to what we can do.

We are part of the dawning of a new day, God's new day, one moment at a time.

Prayer: Jesus, when you tell Peter to put away his sword, you aren't talking to us about how we play; you are showing us another way of living. But two thousand years later, we still haven't learned. We continue to kill others in war, in our homes, and on our streets. We even enjoy pretending to kill people in our play, and actually try to hurt others in sports. But we are beginning to see where all this leads, and we ask your help to turn our lives around—away from violence and fully toward life. Touch us with your gentle spirit. Whether we limit some of this violence as a first step or abstain altogether from violent play and entertainment, help us to sustain our commitment to put more peace in our play.

Reflection: Is reducing or abstaining from violent play and entertainment an appropriate measure for you personally at this time? If so, what will this mean concretely for you? How can you make your play and entertainment as a family or community less violent and more playful?

Songs: "Down By the Riverside" (traditional); "Peace" (Norbet)
Books: *World War Won* by Dave Pilkey (Fresno, CA: Landmark Edns., 1987), WF; *Who's Calling the Shots? How to Respond Effectively to Children's Fascination with War Play and War Toys* by Nancy Carlsson-Paige and Diane Levin (Philadelphia, PA: New Society Publishers, 1990), A; *The Butter Battle Book* by Dr. Seuss (New York: Random House, 1984), WF; *Dana Doesn't Like Guns Anymore* by Carole Moore-Slater (New York: Friendship Press, 1991), WF
Videos: *The War* (a critique of violent play), T/A; other video resources from the Center for Media Literacy (see page 122)

WHY ENCOURAGE VIOLENCE?
DON'T BUY WAR TOYS

7. Play as Creative Performance

Praise [God] with tambourine and dance. (Psalm 150:4)

"You are the light of the world....Let your light shine before others." (Matthew 5:14,16)

My memory of Herbert Von Karajan conducting the Berlin Philharmonic at the Lincoln Center in Washington, DC, in 1963 is richly vivid because the performance was so expressive. His poetic gestures were like ballet with a baton. What a revelation and celebration of divine beauty and creativity! What an act of praise!

But we can derive so much pleasure and express equal praise in our own performances and artistic creations when we combine beauty, grace, dexterity, strength, and strategy—amateurs expressing our gifts and extending our limits. We can derive great pleasure when our children and other young people in our lives express themselves musically, artistically, dramatically, athletically. How sad it is to see television, videos and video games, and other electronic toys rob young people of precious opportunities to create their own play and dramas and enhance their own skills and express themselves creatively.

But there is another dimension to performing arts and sports. Public performance is a critical factor in nurturing compassion and courage, especially in children. Schools in India that are based on Gandhi's philosophy of nonviolent social change include thirty minutes of public performance every day. Each level has its own assembly where students perform in front of their classmates as a way of overcoming their self-consciousness and developing the self-confidence it takes to be an effective public person. This kind of self-confidence is crucial in peacemaking. Breaking up a fight, challenging classmates who are picking on someone, or moving comfortably into situations and groups where people are different (in terms of race, economic class, age, etc.) demand the courage of a sound level of self-confidence.

Presbyterian educator Doug Huneke found something similar in his interviews with three hundred rescuers of Jews during the

Nazi era. He was trying to identify factors in their upbringing that might account for their compassion and courage as adults. Among the ten common characteristics he found was the fact that they all had some experience of public performance as children.

"Talent shows" as a part of family camps and other intergenerational programs are a wonderful opportunity for public performance. They also give everyone a chance to shine and to build a sense of community. These kinds of activities allow us to experience dimensions of ourselves and others that we normally don't— and we grow in mutual respect. Most of all, we give glory to God who delights in our creative use of the gifts we have received.

Prayer: Jesus, you call us to follow you in your public ministry, to let our light shine before others. You ask us to be willing to stand up for others, to speak prophetically, to challenge decision-makers and institutions to reverse their discriminatory, violent, or unjust policies and practices. Help us to challenge ourselves and the young people in our lives to become more expressive and confident through the performing arts, sports, and other forms of public performance.

Reflection: What creative talent(s) do you have that you could enhance and perhaps even "go public" with? How can you encourage public performance as part of the play that members of your family or community engage in?

Songs: "Light One Candle" (Peter, Paul, and Mary); "We Are the Light of the World" (Jean Anthony Greif); "This Little Light of Mine" (African-American spiritual)

Books: *An Outbreak of Peace* by Sarah Pirtle (Santa Cruz, CA: New Society Publishers, 1987; young people become peacemakers in their community through artwork), T/A

Videos: *A Christmas Without Snow* (an amateur choir learns about life while rehearsing "The Messiah"), WF

Part VII
Be Courageous

To challenge violence in all its forms whenever I encounter it, whether at home, at school, at work, or in the community, and to stand with others who are treated unfairly

1. Whenever I Am Weak, I Am Strong

*[God] gives power to the faint, / and strengthens the powerless.
/ ...Those who wait for the LORD shall renew their strength /
...They shall run and not be weary, / they shall walk and not
faint.* (Isaiah 40:29,31)

*"My grace is sufficient for you, for power is made perfect in
weakness."...Whenever I am weak, then I am strong.* (2
Corinthians 12:9-10)

V an Farrington had been a behind-the-scenes person. When
she told me of her struggle to testify before the entire congregation about her commitment to the Family Pledge of Nonviolence, I experienced again the truth of these biblical passages. "I
didn't think I could do it," Van said privately. "But I prayed for
guidance and strength and then I knew I had to speak." Such public testimony was new for Van, but Jesus had touched her and
called her to a heroic level of forgiveness, love, and courage in
embracing the peacemaking mission that emerged from the terrible ordeal of her son's murder.

I, too, have experienced the power of Jesus' guidance and
strength. Years ago, while battling depression, I was asked to lead
a training program for a hundred parish leaders, with a focus on
the US Catholic bishops' 1983 pastoral letter on peace. It seemed
I should accept the invitation, even though I wasn't experiencing
much energy and confidence. I prayed over these passages, put
myself in the hands of Jesus, and asked him to make up for my
weakness and use me as his instrument of peace. I experienced an
extraordinary power during that training program. When it was
over, I could only say, "Thank you, Jesus. Never let me doubt
your presence and power."

When Gandhi was asked how he found the courage to walk
into villages where Hindus and Muslims were slaughtering one
another, he testified that he experienced Jesus walking with him.

This same Jesus walks with us each day. With his power residing within us, nothing should hold us back from embracing the call to be his ambassadors of justice and peace.

Sometimes we experience the power of Jesus and the courage to confront violence and injustice through the presence of others. At other times, Jesus makes his presence and power known to us in our experiences of corporate worship or private prayer. If we open ourselves in prayer to the presence and power of Jesus—before, during, and after any engagement—we will be given the grace to run and not grow weary—and our efforts will likely bear much fruit.

Prayer: Jesus, help me root all my efforts in you. Help me seek your guidance and power in prayer and in the power and discernment that come from the community of peacemaking disciples. Let me not run away from challenges because of my weakness, but rather to see in the weakness a chance for your power to work through me. Thank you for your presence and power in my life.

Reflection: When have you experienced the power of Jesus operating through you, especially in times of weakness? How can you tap into this power deeply and regularly? How can you help others, especially the young people in your life, begin to sense this same power of Jesus in their own lives?

Songs: "Walk With Me" (*Jubilee*, see page 120); "Just a Closer Walk with Thee" (African-American spiritual); "Be Not Afraid" (Bob Dufford); "His Eye Is on the Sparrow" (Civilla Martin)

Books: *I Don't Care* by Marjorie Sharmat (New York: MacMillan, 1977; great pain leads a boy to ask for help), WF; *The Inner Voice of Love* by Henri Nouwen (New York: Doubleday, 1996; journal of Nouwen's "journey through anguish to freedom"), A

Videos: *Romero* and *The Mission* (unarmed pastors walk into violence), T/A

2. Run with Perseverance

But let justice roll down like waters, / and righteousness like an ever-flowing stream. (Amos 5:24)

Therefore, since we are surrounded by so great a cloud of witnesses,...let us run with perseverance the race that is set before us. (Hebrews 12:1)

M any before us have fought the good fight, run with perseverance, and given their lives to overcome violence and injustice. Gandhi, Rosa Parks, Dr. Martin Luther King, Cesar Chavez, Dorothy Day, and millions of other nonviolent drum majors for justice form a sacred cloud of witnesses hovering over us. These people learned the courage to stand against the powers and principalities in each era of history. For, as Paul says in Ephesians, we do not struggle against mere mortals (see 6:10-15). We struggle against the spirit of evil that permeates society in the form of racism, sexism, militarism, materialism, and every other "ism" and phobia that frustrate the fulfillment of God's plan for creation—that we all may be one.

The Spirit of God enables us to resist these powers and principalities by providing us the weapons and armor of truth, justice, and faith in God's own Word and Spirit. Confident that we are part of a unique community of faithful witnesses, we keep our eyes on Jesus who endured to the end and triumphed over the grave. We dare to enter the fray and remain faithful to the end.

One of my heroes in Scripture is the pregnant woman in the Book of Revelation (12:1-2,6). Face to face with a dragon ready to devour her child, the woman dares to issue forth her tiny act of love. Face to face today with the beast of violence, we are asked to summon similar courage and hope and give birth to tiny acts of love and resistance. Hoping against hope, we dare to believe, as Jesus did in the Garden of Gethsemane, that if the seed falls into the ground and dies, it will bear much fruit. We dare believe, as did Jesus and all the prophets before and after him, that life will overcome death and that light will overcome darkness. Rooted in the prophets of old, Martin Luther King put it well: "Truth crushed to earth will rise again. No lie can live forever....I still have a dream, that justice will roll down like water and righteousness like a mighty stream. Men will beat their swords into ploughshares and their spears into pruning hooks. And nation will no longer rise up against nation. Neither shall they study war anymore. I still have a dream."

Prayer: Jesus, like Dr. King and the woman in the Book of Revelation—and in the company of that vast cloud of witnesses encouraging us—help us to keep our eyes on you, to remember your promised presence in every moment, and to run the race to the end. Keep the dream alive, and give us the courage to work to make this dream—your dream—come true.

Reflection: How, where, and when can you rekindle this dream for yourself? How, where, and when can you be more mindful of the company of believers urging you on in the struggle against violence and injustice? What can you do as a family or a community to help make Dr. King's dream come true?

Songs: "We Shall Overcome" (traditional); "Imagine" (John Lennon); "Walking to Bethlehem" (*Jubilee*, see page 120); "The

Impossible Dream" (from *Man of LaMancha*); "There Is a River" (Tim Manion)

Books: *Sweet Clara and the Freedom Quilt* by Deborah Hopkinson (New York: Alfred Knopf, 1993), WF; *Justice Seekers, Peace Makers* and *To Construct Peace* by Michael True (Mystic, CT: Twenty-Third Publications, 1985 and 1992), T/A

Videos: *Gandhi*, T/A; *Long Walk Home* (the Montgomery bus boycott), T/A

3. Courage in the Face of Urban Violence

As he came near and saw the city, he wept over it, saying, "If you...had only recognized on this day the things that make for peace!" (Luke 19:41-42)

To save one life, it is as if you had saved the world. (*Talmud,* quoted in *Peacemaking: Day by Day*, Volume II, page 54)

I was Jason's mentor when he was in elementary school, but it was my first visit to his middle school. As I parked in front of the school, I noticed the garden plot across the street. Later, after noticing a class cross the street to tend the garden, I asked Jason if students regularly cared for the plot. He said, "Yes, it's our enrichment period." When I asked about the origins of the garden, he explained that it is a memorial to one of the neighborhood kids who was killed there in a drive-by shooting. "Enrichment" for these young teens meant tending a garden planted in memory of their slain peer. I remembered Jesus weeping over Jerusalem and a deep sadness invaded my soul.

That sadness invaded our church family several months later when the twenty-five-year-old son of one of our members was similarly gunned down. Later, after taking the Family Pledge of Nonviolence, the mother of the victim shared her courage with the congregation: "Today I have hope—hope because I belong to a committed, spirit-filled faith community; hope because of the families gathered here today to proclaim to God and to you our pledge to live nonviolently in our interactions with each other and others we encounter in our daily lives."

Jesus weeps over our cities as innocent children are killed by gunfire, one every one hundred minutes. But Jesus inspires people like Van to rise above the pain in attempts to stem this tidal wave of violence. Jason, for example, has an entire Presbyterian congregation behind him and forty other young people as part of the "I Have a Dream" Foundation, which began when these kids were fourth graders. Three afternoons a week and three Saturdays a month, Ladue Chapel church members tutor these students and provide a range of enrichment activities. Like Van, these church folk are transforming hurt into hope.

Another Presbyterian Church, this one African-American, partners with a Jewish congregation to provide mentors in the public elementary school near the church. Each team, consisting of one African-American adult and one white adult, works with two students. Barriers of race, class, and religion—as well as the barrier of violence—are being broken down.

Prayer: Jesus, give us your tears of compassion. Help us to see and mourn the violence that is killing children. All children are our children because they are your children. If we have time to help only one child, that one will make a difference. Give us the courage to face our fears and turn our tears into deeds of persistent love. Mary, Mother of Jesus and Mother of the Streets, intercede for all of us.

Reflection: How can you link your life with a child or family facing the risks of violence and poverty? What can your family or community do to challenge the violence in your own community, whether it's gun violence, media violence, school violence, the violence of poverty, racism, or other forms of discrimination?

Songs: "Pass Me Not, O Gentle Savior" (Fanny Crosby); "Let There Be Peace on Earth" (Jackson and Miller); "Blest Are They" (David Haas); "Step By Step" (John McCutcheon)

MOTHER OF THE STREETS

Books: *Disposable Children: America's Child Welfare System* by Renny Golden (Belmont, CA: Wadsworth Publishing Co., 1997), A; *Fist, Stick, Knife, Gun* by Geoffrey Canada (New York: Beacon Press, 1995; the struggle of a boy growing up in urban New York), T/A
Videos: *Boyz 'N the Hood* (the struggle of urban youth), T/A; *Malcolm X* (the confronting of urban violence), T/A

4. The Courage to Challenge Abuse
Thelma Burgonio-Watson

But I call upon God, / and the LORD will save me. / Cast your burden on the LORD, / and [God] will sustain you. (Psalm 55:16,22)

Owe no one anything, except to love one another;..."Love your neighbor as yourself." Love does no wrong to a neighbor. (Romans 13:8,9-10)

After watching the video *Broken Vows: Religious Perspectives on Domestic Violence*, Rosa came to see me. In tearful desperation she told her story of abuse and how her own pastor had doubted her story. Her husband was, the pastor pointed out, a church elder; he certainly wouldn't beat up his wife. As a result, Rosa felt that God and the Church had abandoned her. She felt like the psalmist who cried to God, "Why have you forsaken me?" (22:1).

When we are in crisis, feelings of being abandoned often result from not being believed by those important to us: pastors, family, friends, the Church. But God does not abandoned us. Rather, God hears our lamentation and gives us courage to call the abuser to accountability and to seek support of those who will understand. Such is the story of Rosa.

Rosa was reluctant to tell her story; she believed the abuse was her fault. She felt ashamed and feared that her community would ostracize her. Although she prayed for her husband to change, the abuse continued. She thought if she showed him how much she loved him, he would love her in the same way. Finally, Rosa realized that she couldn't make her husband well, that he needed specialized batterer's counseling. "I knew I had to leave when he hit our daughter," she admitted.

The voices of the survivors in the video empowered Rosa to tell her story to people who understood her experience of abuse. She discovered that she was not alone and that help was available.

Her courage to share her story was the beginning of her journey to seek justice and healing for herself.

It takes courage to confront the violence of abuse—whether you are a victim or an "outsider." Calling abuse hot lines, for example, is not an easy call to make for anyone. Initiating abuse prevention programs at church, in schools, and in youth groups is a challenging task. Some families make their home an emergency safe house for a night or two while long-term shelter is sought. Some faith communities do this also and offer "respite programs" for potential abusers. It all takes courage.

Prayer: Gracious God, open our eyes to the reality of domestic violence. Give us the understanding and compassion to reach out to both victims and survivors. Give us the courage to call those who abuse to accountability and repentance that lead to justice and healing. Help us to love one another as you have shown us in Jesus Christ who came to give life abundantly.

Reflection: Do you, your family, or your faith community reinforce a male dominance that allows abuse in personal relationships? What can you do as a family and/or in your faith community to promote gender equality, to protect victims of spouse abuse and child abuse, and to help stop the abuser's violence? How can your family deal more effectively with "being bullied" at school, at work, at play?

Songs: "There is a Balm in Gilead" (traditional spiritual); "What Does Love Require" (Presbyterian Hymnal, #405); "Let It Be" (Beatles)

Books: *Horton Hears a Who* by Dr. Seuss (New York: Random House, 1954), WF; *Keeping the Faith: Questions and Answers for Abused Women* by Marie M. Fortune (San Francisco: Harper, 1987), A

Videos: *Spitfire Grill* (a husband finally learns to respect his wife), T/A; *Broken Vows: Religious Perspectives on Domestic Violence* (stories of survivors; from CPSDV Productions, see page 120), A

5. Confront the Violence of Poverty

He judged the cause of the poor and needy.... / Is not this to know me? / says the LORD. (Jeremiah 22:16)

"'Just as you did it to one of the least of these who are members of my family, you did it to me.'" (Matthew 25:40)

It wasn't easy for eleven-year-old Trevor Farrell to convince his family to take him to the city streets of Philadelphia to reach out to the homeless people he had seen on television. But he got his entire family involved in what eventually became known as "Trevor's Campaign." From the time he first took to the streets until he graduated from high school, Trevor reached out nightly and discovered a common humanity. It wasn't the homeless shelter he inspired or the thousands of meals he served that touched Trevor the most. It was the friends he made with "people just like me," as he put it, "except that they didn't have money."

In 1984, Jenny Bush-Boyce had a similar encounter after her ninth-grade youth group watched a slide presentation about working with infants in Haiti. There was no way Jenny's physician father was going to allow his daughter to be exposed to such a health risk. After pleading her case for weeks, however, Jenny "won"; her entire family went to Haiti and has returned every year since.

These two youths had the courage to confront the violence of poverty and the good fortune to discover the spiritual wealth of their economically poor friends. The experience of many missionaries confirms the truth that people of faith who go to impoverished areas to evangelize the poor are themselves evangelized by the poor. Divisions of wealth and divisions of spirit go hand in hand.

These same divisions exist in our own country. Many are fearful, for example, to cross those urban boundaries that separate the "haves" from the "have-nots." Many worry about what might happen if they lend their lives to the struggle for economic justice. Where will God lead them? They—we—will be led to the very heart of God. As Jeremiah prophesied, God so identifies with the economically poor and marginalized peoples of our world that we cannot begin to know God until we identify with God's own passion for the poor. Jesus was even more direct: whatever we do to the least, we do to him.

Prayer: Jesus, help us to realize that second-class schools, lack of quality healthcare, inadequate diets, inferior housing, unemployment, and every other aspect of poverty violate the dignity of your people and can kill just as guns do, only in slow motion. Help us break down the barriers that keep us apart. Help us discover our deepest reality—that with you as our brother and God as our Parent, we are all truly sisters and brothers.

Reflection: How can you become more involved in the struggle against the violence of poverty? How can you make this involvement something you can do as a whole family or community?

Songs: "Wonderful World" (*Rainbow People*, see page 120); "The Cry of the Poor" (John Foley); "Brothers and Sisters" (Ziggy Marley); "God of the Hungry" (Scott Soper)

© Fritz Eichenberg Trust/Licensed by VAGA, New York, NY

Books: *Trevor's Place: The Story of the Boy Who Brings Hope to the Homeless* by F. and J. Farrell (New York: Harper and Row, 1990), T/A; *Faces of Poverty: Faces of Christ* by John Kavanaugh and Mev Puleo (Maryknoll, NY: Orbis Books, 1991), T/A; *Amazing Grace: The Lives of Children and the Conscience of A Nation* by Jonathon Kozol (New York: Crown Books, 1995), A
Videos: *Entertaining Angels* (the work of Dorothy Day), T/A

6. Young Ambassadors of Reconciliation

In Christ God was reconciling the world...and entrusting the message of reconciliation to us. So we are ambassadors for Christ. (2 Corinthians 5:19,20)

So it is that the strong are overcome by the weak, the haughty by the humble. This we know but never learn. (Lao Tse, quoted in *Peace Prayers*, page 90)

Ruby Bridges was only six years old when she built bridges in her community. She was the first African-American child to integrate the public schools in her New Orleans neighborhood. Because of parental pressure, her first-grade classmates boycotted school and she was the only one who went, day after day, for an entire year. These same adults, however, did show up to hurl hate words and spit in Ruby's direction before and after school. When asked how she endured, Ruby said that she prayed for her abusers every day, as she approached their gauntlet of hate.

Prietita is only nine when she befriends Joaquin, a shy boy who lives across the Rio Grande from her Texas border town. In this fictional account—in both English and Spanish—Prietita defends Joaquin from the taunts and threats of her older brother and his friends. She experiences the emotional scars of his impoverished existence but is blessed by the generous hospitality of Joaquin's mother. Prietita, her mother, and the community herb woman (healer) hide Joaquin and his mother from the Immigration Patrol. Because of Prietita's courage, the herb woman realizes that she is ready to begin her apprenticeship as the future herb woman.

Angel Perez was only twelve when he became one of the subjects of the video *Young Peacemakers*. This ambassador of reconciliation was trained as a peer mediator in elementary school and is shown speaking to younger students about the courage to be a peer mediator. He recounts how he broke up a fight and showed the two boys how to play cooperatively.

A high school youth group near Lansing, Michigan decided to scrub the steps of the state capitol building after it had been used for a Ku Klux Klan rally. Their symbolic statement spoke clearly to their church as well as to the entire Lansing community.

We may not integrate a school like Ruby Bridges, but we can integrate our lives and challenge segregated structures in our community. We may not be Prietita, but we can welcome immigrants into our lives and our communities, challenge racism and hate words and deeds, and oppose punitive immigration policies. We may not scrub our state capitol steps, but we can join local and national "unity rallies."

Acting courageously in the face of injustice and violence is integral to our faith. We follow a Jesus who found the courage to confront those who would stone a woman and those who would turn a temple of prayer into a den of thieves (see Matthew 21:12-17).

Prayer: Jesus, you reached out compassionately to those your society shunned. Thank you for the many models of youthful courage you raise up in every time in every community. From their example, help us to learn what it means to be ambassadors of reconciliation in our time and community.

Reflection: How can you be an ambassador of reconciliation in your own community? How can you encourage others in your family or community to be ambassadors of reconciliation? Is there some act of reconciliation you could do as an entire group?

Songs: "Sing Praise for the Harvest" (*Jubilee*, see page 120); "Be Not Afraid" (Bob Dufford)
Books: *The Story of Ruby Bridges* by Robert Coles (New York:

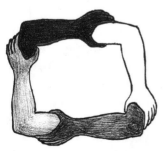

Scholastic Books, 1995), WF; *Friends from the Other Side; Amigos Del Otro Lado* by Gloria Anzaldua (Emeryville, CA: Children's Book Press, 1993), WF
Videos: *Young Peacemakers* (EcuFilm; see page 122), WF; *The War* (a girl defends her Black friend), WF

111

7. Speaking Truth to Power

But if the sentinel sees the sword coming and does not blow the trumpet, so that the people are not warned, and the sword comes and takes any of them,...their blood I will require at the sentinel's hand. (Ezekiel 33:6)

"'My house shall be called a house of prayer'; / but you are making it a den of robbers." (Matthew 21:13)

Just as the Hebrew prophets challenge the powerful of their times, Jesus chastises the merchants in the Temple. To emphasize his truth, he overturns their tables and scatters their money and wares.

Clearly, there are times to use words and actions to unmask injustice and violence. United States President Eisenhower, for example, tried to warn his country with these words: "Every gun that is made, every warship launched, every rocket fired, signifies...a theft from those who hunger and are not fed, those who are cold and not clothed" (April 6, 1953). Like the prophet Ezekiel, Eisenhower saw a sword coming—an escalating arms race—and sounded his trumpet to warn the people.

While we can't address whole nations, God has posted us as sentinels for others. If we see a sword coming—violent shows, legislation stripping people of basic needs, repeal of gun-control ordinances, cutbacks in enrichment programs for urban schools, elimination of jobs or recreation opportunities for poor youth—we are called to sound our trumpets and warn the people.

Lindsay Graham came to the United Sates from England in 1992, after seeing a documentary film on the life of Alan Bannister, a death row inmate since 1983. She worked tirelessly on his behalf, trying to get him a new trial. Month after month, she confronted the governor and attorney-general of Missouri, with temporary success. On December 6, 1994, the Supreme Court granted Alan a stay of execution just two hours before he was to be executed. Thirty-four more months of organizing and lobbying state officials did not succeed in getting Alan a new trial, however; Alan Bannister was executed on October 22, 1997.

Lindsay lost, true, but that's not the ultimate truth. Her support of Alan helped him write a book about the death penalty. Who knows what has happened in the souls of the state officials and prison authorities she confronted with her courage and constancy. Lindsay and Alan mobilized thousands of people who will probably resist the death penalty with more courage and constancy precisely because of their example.

Prayer: All powerful and ever-loving God, you raised up many Hebrew prophets to warn your people of violence and injustice. Then you gave us Jesus to show us the way and the truth and the life. Jesus, you teach us that there are times when we must speak and act on behalf of truth and those in need. You inspire millions, who in turn inspire us. Help us find the courage to follow in your and their prophetic footsteps.

Reflection: What "sword" do you see coming and for what portion of God's people can you sound your trumpet? What group or individuals can you link with to make the sound of your trumpet more effective? Is there some prophetic action against injustice that your family or community could participate in?

Songs: "Here I Am, Lord" (Dan Schutte); "Jubilee" (*Jubilee*, see page 120); "Well May the World" (Pete Seeger)
Books: *It's Our World, Too!* by Phillip Hoose (Boston, MA: Little, Brown and Co., 1993; stories of youth who have challenged social evils), T/A
Videos: *Mother of the Year* (see page 120, the story of a woman

speaking truth to power and passing on her passion to her children and grandchildren), T/A; *Silkwood* (a nuclear plant worker confronts her company), T/A; *Marie* (a state official confronts the governor over corruption), T/A

8. In the Face of Escalating Violence, Escalate Love

The light shines in the darkness, and the darkness did not overcome it. (John 1:5)

"Take courage; I have conquered the world!" (John 16:33)

My true religion is kindness. (Dalai Lama, quoted in *Peacemaking: Day by Day*, Volume II, page 133)

Some forms of violence are hard to counteract. There are thousands of violent situations every day, for example, that we can do nothing about. But this need not lead us to despair or paralysis. In fact, I like to view the struggle between love and violence as two scales, one loaded with the boulders of violence (war, rape, murder, racism, sexism, greed) and the other filled with millions of tiny pebbles, each an act of love.

At the outbreak of the Persian Gulf War in January 1991, a phrase came to me that continues to orient my life: In the face of escalating violence, escalate love. I could not stop that war, though I wrote many letters, gave many talks, protested publicly with others many times. What I felt I could do to offset that massive violence was to escalate the number of random acts of kindness I committed. In the process, I learned lots of possibilities from others:

- Put people's newspapers on their front porches with a prayer during a neighborhood walk.
- Write anonymous notes of appreciation to neighbors who beautify the neighborhood with their flowers or to individuals doing good things.
- Help a motorist or traveler in distress.
- Greet strangers on the street, in the store, on the elevator with a friendly word and a smile.

Each kind word and deed, each smile, each surprise gift, each sacrifice, adds up to many pebbles on the scale of love.

Keep in mind that it's not the quantity of such deeds but the quality of each deed. My model for years has been Sadako Sasaki and her tiny act of generosity—making her 644th and final paper crane with all the energy she had left in her dying body. She wrote "peace" on its wings as a plea to the world to prevent other children from dying in atomic/nuclear war. Sadako's last crane inspired her classmates in Hiroshima to finish the remaining 356 cranes, to reach her original goal of 1000. Later her classmates raised funds to build a memorial to her. Within a few years, a thirty-foot arch, topped with a statue of Sadako holding a crane over her head, was completed in the Peace Park in Hiroshima. Children all over the world send strands of paper cranes to be hung from the arch. Hundreds of children in the United States spent five years (1990-1995) on a project to match the Hiroshima arch with a peace sculpture in New Mexico. Paper cranes are entering prisons, hospitals, and places of hospice, reminding recipients to make the most of whatever moments they have—as Sadako did.

Prayer: Jesus, help us to give ourselves as fully and lovingly as we can, wherever we can, for as long as we can. Multiply our random acts of kindness. Rekindle our hope that your light has truly overcome the darkness; that love, not violence, is the last word; and that we shall overcome someday.

Reflection: How can you escalate love this week; every week? How can you incorporate Sadako's spirit into your family and bring that spirit to others?

Songs: "All I Really Need" (*Rainbow People*, see page 120); "Perhaps Love" (John Denver); "If We Only Have Love" (Jacques Berel)
Books: *Sadako and the Thousand Paper Cranes* by Eleanor Coerr (NY: Putnam, 1977), WF; *An Interrupted Life* by Etty Hillesum (New York: Pocket Books, 1991), T/A
Videos: *Romero* (escalating love in El Salvador), T/A

VIOLENCE

LOVE

9. The Power of the Cross

"Unless a grain of wheat falls into the earth and dies, it re-mains just a single grain; but if it dies, it bears much fruit." (John 12:24)

"If any want to become my followers, let them deny themselves and take up their cross and follow me." (Mark 8:34)

When Jesus dares to proclaim a new "Way" of living that threatens the Roman Empire, he is crucified. But Jesus triumphs over death and transforms the cross from a symbol of violence into the way by which violence is overcome. Through Jesus, God shows us that the acceptance of death by the oppressive powers of this violent world is actually the unleashing of an even greater power.

The fire of God's transforming love spreads through the early Christian community, and the Roman Empire cannot put it out. It ignites in Gandhi and spreads through the Indian people in both South Africa and India, and the British Empire cannot put it out. It ignites in Rosa Parks and spreads through Montgomery, Alabama, and the white power structure cannot put it out. It ignites in Dr. Martin Luther King, Jean Donovan, Oscar Romero, and thousands of others, and the powers of oppression and violence cannot put it out. They kill Donovan, Romero, Gandhi, King, Jesus—but the fire of love spreads all the more intensely. As Archbishop Romero put it two weeks before his death, "If they kill me, I shall arise in the Salvadoran people."

Perhaps we can best identify with Jean Donovan. This successful American businesswoman leaves the "good life" to work with the poor in El Salvador. As the situation becomes dangerous, her family and friends urge her to leave. She is tempted but, because she has come to so love the children, she simply cannot leave. She is martyred on December 2, 1980. As Jean's seed falls into the ground and dies, however, it bears much fruit. Her fire spreads and touches all who knew her—and millions more.

We are called to take up the cross and follow Jesus—perhaps

116

not as dramatically, but every bit as generously as the martyrs did. We die to ourselves daily when we listen, forgive, stand with victims of hate, violence, or poverty, and challenge policy makers in government, corporations, and other institutions—all with love. It's not the dramatic death of martyrdom, but it is the faithful dying to self, day after day, year after year, that knows no "retirement." God's transforming power of love ignites in us and spreads through the circles of our lives and the generations that follow.

Prayer: Jesus, help us to take up the cross and follow you. May we be willing to sacrifice our time, our comfort, our privileges, our wealth, our position, and our reputation for the victims of violence and injustice. Deepen our courage and faith.

Reflection: Have you ever experienced this kind of "dying"? With what results (fruit)? How is Jesus asking you to "fall into the ground and die" in confronting the powers of violence at this moment in your life? What risks are your family or community willing to take to stand against the violence and injustices of our time?

Songs: "Where Two or Three Gather" and "O Come And Mourn" (*Jubilee*, see page 120); "Lord of the Dance" (Shaker song)
Books: *Salvador Witness* by Ana Carrigan (New York: Ballantine Books, 1986; a biography of Jean Donovan), T/A; *Dreaming God's Dream* by Kathleen McGinnis (Baptist Peace Fellowship, 1990; family activities on Martin Luther King), WF; *The Nonviolent Coming of God* by James Douglass (Maryknoll, NY: Orbis Books, 1991; the biblical and social analysis behind this meditation), A
Videos: *Romero*, T/A; *The Mission* (missionaries resist the oppression of indigenous people in Latin America), T/A; *A Dangerous Life* (nonviolent resistance to Marcos in the Philippines), T/A

Families Against Violence Advocacy Network and the Family Pledge of Nonviolence

The Families Against Violence Advocacy Network (FAVAN) was launched in March 1996. Fifty representatives of national organizations, most Christian denominations, and other faith traditions gathered in St. Louis, Missouri, at the invitation of the Parenting for Peace and Justice Network of the Institute for Peace and Justice. These people committed themselves to work together on a comprehensive campaign that would address the violence in North America. Over the next twelve months, there evolved a five-step effort to break the cycle of violence.

Step 1 calls for taking the Family (or School) Pledge of Nonviolence for families, faith communities, and students (see page xii).

Step 2 calls for finding ways to support those taking the Pledge. This effort continues in the forming of family support groups and other circles of peace, and creating resources for faith communities and schools to teach the Pledge.

Step 3 calls for spreading the Pledge. This effort continues as the Pledge is translated into other languages and is adapted for use throughout the world and in every major faith tradition, as are the accompanying resources for living the Pledge. For example, the Pledge is being given to healthcare, day-care, and other social service providers; to parent educators and Head Start teachers; and to many others who interact with children and families.

Step 4 calls for helping local communities organize to address the many different manifestations of violence in their communities. This effort continues as FAVAN leaders and teams bring together already existing violence prevention groups and invite local families, individuals, and faith communities to join these efforts.

Step 5 calls for linking these local efforts with national advocacy organizations and campaigns that focus on the issues of gun violence, media violence, violence in schools, the violence of poverty, domestic violence, and hate violence.

The short-term goal in these steps is to have one million families and ten thousand schools committed to the Pledge by the year 2000, FAVAN teams established in hundreds of cities throughout the nation, a national advocacy effort involving at least one thousand national organizations as well as tens of thousands of local organizations, and similar efforts in other countries. We have joined the Nobel Peace Laureates in their campaign to make 2000 the "Year for the Education of Nonviolence." At the beginning of the new millennium, we want to join with the Laureates in making 2000-2010 a "Decade for the Culture of Nonviolence" and launch a "Century of Nonviolence," around the world.

This is an enormous task. But as we state in the FAVAN Manifesto, "In the face of widespread violence, many people are frightened, confused, frustrated, angry, and, perhaps worst, feeling powerless. We, however, claim both a power and responsibility to respond. We join together in this Advocacy Network to express a moral voice, a voice of outrage, that calls all families and our whole culture to reject violence and violent 'solutions' to problems. We will break the cycle of violence by creating a circle of families who can be strong and bold because we stand together. We say 'NO!' to violence in our homes, and 'YES!' to countering violence and promoting alternatives to violence in our communities and world."

Please join us!

119

Resources from the Institute for Peace and Justice

Videos and Audio Cassettes

Teaching Peace by Red Grammer

Rainbow People by Susan Stark

Jubilee by Jean and Jim Strathdee

Mother of the Year video (rental only)

Books

Just Family Nights by Susan Vogt (Elgin, IL: Brethren Press, 1994)

Earth Prayers from Around the World, Elizabeth Roberts, editor (San Francisco, CA: Harper and Row, 1991)

Families Valued by Jack Nelson-Pallmeyer (New York: Friendship Press, 1996)

FAVAN Resources

Families Creating a Circle of Peace by James McGinnis, Jim Vogt, Ken Lovingood, and Gretchen Lovingood: a forty-page booklet of stories, cartoons, family activities, and other resources for implementing the Family Pledge of Nonviolence. Also available in Spanish: *Familias Creando un Circulo de Paz.*

Creating Circles of Peace: Alternatives to Violence Kits: for Christian churches (available in English and Spanish), for Christian education programs/schools, for public school grades K-5, and for public school grades 6-12.

Circles of Hope, Circles of Peace by LaDoris Payne-Bell: a thirty-two-page leader's handbook about empowering families to deal with poverty, violence, and other social forces impacting families, especially lower-income families; with a participant's booklet on the Family Pledge of Nonviolence.

"Circles of Peace, Circles of Justice": a bi-monthly newsletter for families and communities on implementing the themes of the Family Pledge of Nonviolence; includes a four-page "FAVAN Update," suggesting action, resources, and organizing strategies around the Pledge.

For a catalog and further information, contact
4144 Lindell Blvd., #408
St. Louis, Missouri 63108
314-533-4445
fax: 314-533-1017
e-mail: ppjn@aol.com
website: http://members.aol.com/ppjn

Other Groups for Resources and Action

Bridge Building Images (P.O. Box 1048, Burlington, VT 05402; 1-800-325-6263; www.wowpages.com/bbi) will provide a catalog of their greeting cards, posters, and other iconographic visuals.

Center for Media Literacy (4727 Wilshire Blvd., #403, Los Angeles, CA 90010; 1-800-226-9494; e-mail: cml@earthlink.net) has an excellent video program for developing critical viewing skills.

Center for the Prevention of Sexual and Domestic Violence (936 N. 34th St., Suite 200, Seattle, WA 98103; 206-634-1903; e-mail: cpsdv@cpsdv.org) offers books, videos, training, and consultation on abuse prevention, domestic violence, child abuse, sexual violence, and clergy misconduct.

Children's Book Press (6400 Hollis St., #4, Emeryville, CA 94608) offers children's books related to violence and abuse.

EcuFilm (810 12th Ave. South, Nashville, TN 37203; 1-800-251-4091) offers *Young Peacemakers* and other related videos.

Fellowship of Reconciliation (P.O. Box 271, Nyack, NY 10960; 914-358-4601) offers books, greeting cards, *Fellowship* magazine, and faith-based "Peace Fellowship" networks.

Global Education Associates (475 Riverside Dr., New York, NY 10115) offers copies of the "Earth Covenant," provides global networks and projects, and publishes books and *Breakthrough* magazine.

Maryknoll Foreign Mission Society (Maryknoll, NY 10545; 1-800-258-5838) offers *Maryknoll* magazine, Orbis Books, and related videos.

Mennonite Media Productions (1251 Virginia Ave., Harrisonburg, VA 22801; 1-800-999-3534) offers *Murder Close Up* and related videos.

Pax Christi USA (532 W. 8th St., Erie, PA 16502; 814-453-4955) offers a catalog of their books, greeting cards, posters; "Catholic Peace Voice" tabloid, and membership and action options.

Visual Parables (P.O. Box 58, Topeka, KS 66601-0058; 1-800-528-6522) offers a monthly magazine of Christian reflections on films and videos by Dr. Edward McNulty.

Sources for Inspirational Passages

Mary Lou Kownacki, editor, *Peacemaking: Day by Day*, Volumes I and II (Erie, PA: Pax Christi, 1985 & 1989)

Thich Nhat Hanh, *Present Moment, Wonderful Moment* and *Mindfulness* as well as other books on meditations from a Buddhist perspective (Parallax Press, P.O. Box 7355; Berkeley, CA 94707; 510-525-0101)

Murray Polner et al, editor, *The Challenge of Shalom* (Philadelphia, PA: New Society Publishers, 1994; also available from the Jewish Peace Fellowship at the Fellowship of Reconciliation, P.O. Box 271, Nyack, NY 10960; 914-358-4601)

Glenn Paige et al, editor, *Islam and Nonviolence* (Honolulu, HI: University of Hawaii, 1993; also available from the Muslim Peace Fellowship at the Fellowship of Reconciliation, P.O. Box 271, Nyack, NY 10960; 914-358-4601)

Elizabeth Roberts, editor, *Earth Prayers from Around the World* (San Francisco, CA: Harper and Row, 1991; also available from the Institute for Peace and Justice)

Stephen B. Scharper and Hilary Cunningham, editors, *The Green Bible* (Maryknoll, NY: Orbis Books, 1993)

Contributors

Authors

Thelma Burgonio-Watson is a Presbyterian minister and a program specialist at the Center for the Prevention of Sexual and Domestic Violence in Seattle, Washington.

Gloria Green is a prayer leader and the director of the St. Charles Lwanga Center, a center for African-American spirituality in St. Louis, Missouri.

Nancy Hastings Sehested is an itinerant preacher, retreat leader, and the pastor of the Sweet Fellowship Baptist Church in Clyde, North Carolina.

Ken Lovingood is an African-American husband, father, poet, workshop leader, co-author of several books for families, and peace activist residing in Santa Barbara, California.

Jim McGinnis is a workshop and retreat leader. He and his wife, Kathy, are the authors of many books for teachers and families and are the directors of the Institute for Peace and Justice in St. Louis, Missouri.

Don Mosley is the co-founder of Jubilee Partners, a Christian service community in Comer, Georgia, a lifelong peace and justice activist, and author of *With Our Own Eyes*.

Palmira Perea-Hay is a native New Mexican. She and her husband, Steve, are social workers with Catholic Family Services in Lubbock, Texas.

Other Contributors

Kass Dotterweich is the editor of this book. Her careful and thoughtful guidance made the whole process an act of love and prayer for all involved.

Susan Crowe is an art teacher at St. Paul's School in Fenton, Missouri. Susan, along with her daughter, Angela, and several of her students, provided a great deal of original art for this work.

Other contributing artists: Sister Renee de Porres Fenner; Helen David Brancato, IHM; Gen Cassani, SSND; Linda French Griffin; Catherine Martin, O.Carm.; Mary Lee Rovira; Grady Gunter; Fritz Eichenberg; and Robert Lentz (see pages 127-128 for specific credits)

Songs: Suggested by Jim Ford and Arlecia Stamps

Videos: Suggested by Edward McNulty

Readers: Esther Armstrong, Jean Chapman, Jim Douglass, Rabbi Jim Goodman, Kathy McGinnis, Dot Savage, and Dale Stitt

Credits and Permissions

Page viii: Artwork by Michael Patrick Openlander

Page 3: Artwork by Susan Crowe

Page 5: Artwork by Angela Crowe (age 15)

Page 7: Artwork by Sister Renee de Porres Fenner

Page 9: Artwork by Gen Cassani

Page 11: Artwork by Susan Crowe

Page 13: Artwork by Grady Gunter

Page 15: Photo of Rosa Parks receiving the Peace Abbey Courage of Conscience Award at JFK Library and Museum in Boston MA, 1992, used with permission

Page 19: Artwork by Susan Crowe

Page 21: Artwork by Sister Renee de Porres Fenner

Page 23: Artwork by Susan Crowe

Page 25: Artwork by Krystle Mainini (age 12)

Page 27: Artwork by Susan Crowe

Page 29: Artwork by Mary Lee Rovira

Page 35: Artwork by Sister Renee de Porres Fenner

Page 37: Artwork by Susan Crowe

Page 39: Artwork by Lauren Burkhardt (age 10)

Page 41: Artwork by Sister Renee de Porres Fenner

Page 43: Artwork by Susan Crowe

Page 45: Artwork by Sister Renee de Porres Fenner

Page 51: Artwork by Susan Crowe

Page 53: Photography by Jim McGinnis

Page 55: Artwork by Susan Crowe

Page 57: Artwork by Susan Crowe

Page 59: Artwork by Sister Renee de Porres Fenner

Page 61: Artwork by Susan Crowe

Page 63: "Christ of the Americas" created by Sister Helen David Brancato for Maryknoll, used with permission

Page 67: Artwork by Kristen Strubberg (age 11)

Page 69: Artwork by Pax Christi, USA, used with permission

Page 71: Photography by Jim McGinnis

Page 73: Photography by Jim McGinnis

Page 75: Artwork by Helen David Brancato, appearing in *Peacemaking: Day by Day,* Volume I, used with permission
Page 77: Artwork by Gen Cassani, used with permission
Page 79: Artwork by Sister Renee de Porres Fenner
Page 81: Artwork by Linda French Griffin and the "World Pledge" by Lillian Genser (Women's International League for Peace and Freedom), as it appears in *Seeds of Peace,* New Haven, CT: New Society Publishers, used with permission of publisher, author, and artist
Page 85: Artwork by Helen David Brancato, appearing in *Peacemaking: Day by Day,* Volume I, used with permission
Page 87: Photography by Jim McGinnis
Page 89: Artwork by Anna Marshall (age 12)
Page 91: Artwork by Susan Crowe
Page 93: Artwork by Susan Crowe
Page 95: Used with permission from Donnelly/Colt (Stop War Toys Campaign, Box 1093, Norwich, CT 06360)
Page 97: Artwork by Susan Crowe
Page 101: Artwork by Sister Renee de Porres Fenner
Page 103: "Prophets of Nonviolence" by Sister Catherine Martin, O. Carm., used with permission from the artist
Page 105: "Mother of the Streets" by Robert Lentz; © 1986, Robert Lentz, used with permission of Bridge Building Images, P.O. Box 1048, Burlington, VT 05402
Page 107: Logo designed by the Presbyterian Church (USA) team working on the Societal Violence Initiative: Confronting Violence Against Women, used with permission
Page 109: "The Lord's Supper" by Fritz Eichenberg; © Fritz Eichenberg Trust/Licensed by VAGA, New York: NY, used with permission
Page 111: Artwork by Susan Crowe
Page 113: Photography by Mev Puleo, used with permission
Page 115: Artwork by Joshua Crowe (age 18)
Page 117: Artwork by Sister Renee de Porres Fenner